NATIONALITY IN MODERN HISTORY

THE MACMILLAN COMPANY
NEW YORK · BOSTON · CHICAGO · DALLAS
ATLANTA · SAN FRANCISCO

MACMILLAN & CO., Limited
LONDON · BOMBAY · CALCUTTA
MELBOURNE

THE MACMILLAN CO. OF CANADA, Ltd.
TORONTO

NATIONALITY IN MODERN HISTORY

BY

J. HOLLAND ROSE, Litt.D.

FELLOW OF CHRIST'S COLLEGE, CAMBRIDGE
READER IN MODERN HISTORY TO THE UNIVERSITY OF CAMBRIDGE
CORRESPONDING MEMBER OF THE MASSACHUSETTS HISTORICAL SOCIETY

" Avoir fait de grandes choses ensemble, vouloir en
faire encore, voilà la condition essentielle pour être un
peuple."—RENAN.

New York
THE MACMILLAN COMPANY
1916

PREFACE

Lectures I–VIII of this series were delivered at Cambridge in the Michaelmas Term of 1915; and Lectures IX and X are based on those which I delivered in December last to the Historical Associations at Birmingham and Bristol. My aim throughout has been historical, namely, to study the varied manifestations of Nationality among the chief European peoples, before attempting to analyze or define it. That I have sought to do in Lecture VIII. It is noteworthy that only in recent times has Nationality become a conscious and definite movement. Apart from the writings of Machiavelli, where that instinct figures dimly, it was not (I believe) treated by any writer before the year 1758. Then an anonymous Swiss brought out a book entitled "Von dem Nationalstolze" (*Of National Pride*), in which he discussed its good and bad characteristics. I have no space in which to summarize his work; but at some points it breathes the spirit of Schiller's *Wilhelm Tell*, the inner meaning of which I have sought to portray in Lecture III.

I began these studies several years ago, and early in 1916 was about to complete them. Most of my conclusions have not been modified by the present war; but the questions discussed in the later lectures arise out of that conflict. There, as elsewhere, I hope, my treatment has been as objective and impartial as present conditions admit. Lack of space has precluded a study of the lesser national movements in Europe and of all similar movements outside of Europe. I regret this latter omission because the growth of Nationality in the United States and the British Commonwealths is developing a wider and cosmopolitan sentiment which makes for peace.

At present, however, we are confronted by Nationality of the old type; and to pass it by with sneers as to its being antiquated does not further the international cause. A careful study of past and present conditions is the first requisite for success in the construction of the healthier European polity which ought to emerge from the present conflict; and criticisms of German Socialists such as will be found in Lectures IX and X, are, I believe, necessary if mankind is to avoid a repetition of the disastrous blunders of July, 1914.

The sense which I attach to the words "race," "people," "nation," "nationality," "nationalism," is, briefly, as follows: For the reasons stated in Lecture VIII, I have rarely used the word "race," and then only as a quasi-scientific term. The word "people" I have generally used as implying a close sense of kinship; "nation" as a political term, designating a people which has attained to state organization; "nationality" (in the concrete sense) as a people which has not yet attained to it; but I have nearly always referred to "Nationality," in the ideal sense, namely, as an aspiration towards united national existence. In Lecture IX I have used "Nationalism" to denote the intolerant and aggressive instinct which has of late developed in Germany and the Balkan States.

My thanks are due to Professor Bury, Litt. D. Regius Professor of Modern History in the University of Cambridge; to Professor Deschamps of the Institut supérieur de Commerce of Antwerp (now resident in Cambridge); to Mr. G. P. Gooch, M. A., formerly Scholar of Trinity College, Cambridge; and to Mr. A. B. Hinds, M. A., formerly Student of Christ Church, Oxford, for their valued advice and criticism.

J. H. R.

February, 1916.

TABLE OF CONTENTS

LECTURE I

THE DAWN OF THE NATIONAL IDEA

LECTURE II

VIVE LA NATION

LECTURE III

SCHILLER AND FICHTE

vii

LECTURE IV

THE SPANISH NATIONAL RISING

LECTURE V

MAZZINI AND YOUNG ITALY

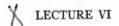

LECTURE VI

THE AWAKENING OF THE SLAVS

LECTURE VII

THE GERMAN THEORY OF THE STATE

LECTURE VIII

NATIONALITY AND MILITARISM

LECTURE IX

NATIONALISM SINCE 1885

LECTURE X

INTERNATIONALISM

NATIONALITY IN MODERN HISTORY

NATIONALITY IN MODERN HISTORY

LECTURE I

THE DAWN OF THE NATIONAL IDEA

It is well sometimes to do with the map of Europe at critical periods what a painter does with his canvas, stand away from it and view it with half-closed eyes so as to behold only the salient features. What is the impression produced by the Europe of the Roman Empire of 1800 years ago? Solidity and universality are its characteristics. Eight hundred years later the scene is changed to one of chaos. The attempt of the rulers of the Holy Roman Empire to achieve unity has failed and civilization is lost in a medley of little domains. By slow degrees these sort themselves out, like to like for the most part; and by the year 1600 the outlines of large States are clearly defined, especially in the West of Europe. Italy and Germany are minutely divided; and the inroads of the Turks have worked havoc in the South-East. Still, Europe is settling down on a new basis; and not even the Wars of Religion long delay the assorting process except in Germany. The political bioscope continues to shift until there emerge large blocks of territory which tend to absorb the smaller areas. The Napoleonic Wars and the series of modern wars beginning in 1859 complete this solidifying work; and only in the South-East of Europe do we find a great Empire splitting up into smaller parts. Elsewhere, the contrary is the case; and in 1878–1914 Europe consists of solid blocks, which stoutly resist every attempt to break them up.

To resume; in the old Roman times Europe forms a solid whole. In the fifth century it splits up into small areas; and the period of small areas and fleeting States continues far into the Middle Ages; but by slow degrees these minute sub-divisions lessen in number and increase in size; until, in the nineteenth and early twentieth centuries, the map of Europe acquires a clearness and consistency never known since the time of the old Roman Empire. First, there is unity; then chaos; then an approach to simplicity and solidity.

If we inquire into the causes of these very striking changes we come to these general conclusions: The unity of the Roman world was due to its conquest by a single State, which possessed a far greater military and political efficiency than that developed by other peoples. Therefore they were absorbed by it, until, on the break up of that wonderful organism, there ensued utter confusion, the natural result of unchecked racial strifes. The chaos became semi-organic during the Middle Ages, and at their close another influence began to operate, which grouped together the units and brought them into ever larger masses. These masses are the modern States. Now, what has been the influence most conducive to State-building? That, I hope, we shall discover in this course of lectures.

This brief survey will have shown that some mighty influence has been at work in the modern world far different from anything that was known to the ancients. In Europe and on its confines there was no State that was conterminous with a great people. Assyria, Persia, and Egypt held sway over several peoples alien to the ruling race; and the Mogul Empire was a mere conglomerate. But there was one exception, small in extent but infinitely interesting. The Jews during some generations formed a single compact national

State. With the possible exceptions of China and Babylon they are the first example of a nation in the modern sense. Their records show the rise of the family into the tribe, of the tribe into the nation; and for a time the nation was held together by a strong instinct of kinship. The union was sanctified and strengthened by religious rites and by a profound sense of consecration to the Deity. Thus there came about a sense of unity which held together a singularly stiff-necked, clannish people; and there grew up that spiritual and moral fellowship which has survived eighteen centuries of dispersion. True, the Jews did not long hold together politically. But, despite the disruptive tendencies of their degenerate days, they remained and still remain one at heart. The consciousness of being "the chosen people" still unites them, whether they dwell in the mansions of Paris and New York, or vegetate in the slums of Warsaw and Lisbon, or practise their ancient rites in the valleys of Abyssinia. Israel is still a moral and religious unit, inspired by the most tenacious sense of kinship known to history.

Elsewhere in the Ancient World there was no State that can be called national, at least not in Europe. The Greeks never achieved political union. Thrilled though they were by their legendary epic, and inspired at times by the worship of Ζεὺς ὁ πανελλήνιος, they very rarely joined in defence of their peninsula. Only when the Persians covered the plains of Thessaly did the Greeks make common cause; and then the union was brief and doubtful. For all their scorn of other peoples as barbarians, for all their care in excluding non-Greeks from the Olympian and other great festivals, they often sided with aliens against their own kith and kin. The patriotic appeals of Demosthenes failed to unite them against Philip of Macedon; and they fell, because at bottom their political system was not national, only municipal. City fought with city; and never at the supreme crisis did the

City-States effectively unite. The Greek polity stopped short at the city or the clan. Except in regard to religion, art and athletics it never attained to nationality.[1]

Very different is the history of Rome. Her people, though far less imaginative than those of Athens, possessed the political gifts needful for the upbuilding of a Commonwealth. Rome early absorbed other cities; she then absorbed the Samnites, the Greeks of South Italy and the Gauls of the North. After unifying Italy, she went far towards unifying the then known world. From the Clyde to the Euphrates, from the Tagus to the Rhine, she moulded diverse tribes and formed an almost universal State. As Professor Reid[2] has shown, she accomplished this wonderful feat largely by the grant of wide municipal liberties, thereby welding into her imperial system the City-States which Greek separatism had failed to unite. Besides tactful toleration in local affairs, Imperial Rome displayed a peculiar attractive power which drew aliens into her polity; and in this faculty of assimilation lay her chief strength. Vergil proclaimed that it was her mission to crush the proud and spare those who submitted. The latter process is more important than mere conquest. Indeed, the only real conquest is that which assimilates the conquered. All other triumphs are vain and evanescent. Now, Rome had this absorbing power to a unique degree. The Jews and Greeks were exclusive and intolerant towards Gentiles and barbarians. Not so the Roman. He brought the conquered within the pale; he adopted their deities,[3]

---

[1] The Amphictyonic Council was the only Pan-Hellenic institution; but it rarely acted with vigor. Isocrates desired to unite all Greece with Philip of Macedon for the invasion of Asia; but Demosthenes and nearly all Athenians scouted the scheme.

[2] J. S. Reid, *Municipalities in the Roman Empire*.

[3] See the complaint of Juvenal [III, 60]:

'Jam pridem Syrus in Tiberim defluxit Orontes."

he enrolled their warriors and made them proud of fighting under the eagles, until it seemed possible that tribalism would vanish from Europe and that the world would become Roman.

It was not to be. Other barbarian tribes, obeying some unknown but potent impulse, burst into the imperial domain; and civilization reeled back into the tribal stage from which Rome had raised it. The political unity of Europe vanished; and the human race has never again been able to realize the homogeneity attained by Imperial Rome. During the Dark Ages the annals of mankind became pettily local. Nevertheless, amidst those bewildering shiftings to and fro, racial settlements of the utmost importance were taking place. Indeed, since the year 1000, few ethnical changes of any moment have occurred, if we except the Norman settlements, the incursion of the Turks and the expulsion of the Moors. With those exceptions the groupings of the European peoples of to-day are discernible at that date; and the course of events, especially during the last fifty years has tended to identify more or less closely the political frontiers with the bounds of the habitations marked out by the great European peoples during the long and obscure struggles of the Dark Ages. As will appear in the sequel, some peoples, possessing greater attractive or organizing power, have gained at the expense of others less gifted or energetic; but in their broad outlines the great States of to-day recall those of the chief settlements consequent on the Wanderings of the Peoples.

How came it that the binding influences of Christianity and the haunting memories of the old Roman Empire did not group together in a solid polity the barbarous tribes that then overran Europe? The triumph of Christianity over paganism was swift and complete; and even the proudest and fiercest of the barbarians venerated Rome and her laws. But during the Middle Ages the city which had united the Ancient World became the source of disunion. The successors of St. Peter contended for supremacy with the heirs of the Cæsars, with results fatal both to the Papacy and to the Holy Roman Empire. Institutions which claimed a dominion as wide as Christendom were rent by schism and faction; and both lost in vitality owing to the intolerable strain.

During the struggle the first glimmerings of national consciousness become visible. In their struggle for Temporal Power Hildebrand and his successors at the Vatican could rarely rely on armed support outside Italy. The wavering fortunes of the Empire were sustained in the main by Germans. Yet the struggle never became national in the modern sense. The Popes could always range many a German duchy against its Emperor; and he embattled not a few Italian cities against the Vatican, even when the Lombard League formed its sure bulwark in the North. Thus, clashing claims of world-supremacy were sustained by forces that were not even national; and to this cross division of forces, as well as of ideals, the wretched welter of Germany and Italy in the Middle Ages may largely be ascribed. *Weltpolitik* cannot succeed unless its foundations are both extensive and solid. Both Pope and Emperor sought to found their polities on a basis no less shifting than narrow.

Against this perversion of a divine mission and of a national duty the first great political thinker of the Middle Ages uttered a solemn protest. Dante, no less a statesman and patriot than a poet and seer, protested against the schism to which Italy and Germany were a prey; and in the course of his protests he uttered words which foretold the future glory of the Roman people. The challenge to action rings through the verses in which he bewails the degradation of his land:—

"Ah, slavish Italy! Thou inn of griefs!
Vessel without a pilot in loud storm!
No mistress of fair provinces,
But brothel-house impure!

.   .   .   .

Ah people! Thou obedient still shouldst live
And in thy saddle let thy Cæsar sit
If well thou markedst that which God commands."

And then he appeals to the Emperor, Albert I, to come and
claim his due:—

"Come and behold thy Rome, who calls on thee,
Desolate widow, day and night, with moans—
'My Cæsar, why dost thou desert my side?
Come and behold what love among thy people.'" [1]

For these and the like utterances Dante has been dubbed
a Ghibelline. He was more Ghibelline than Guelf; but
in truth he was a farseeing patriot who sought to reconcile
the Empire and the Papacy, thereby assuring peace to Italy
and order to the world.

Such is the theme of his chief political work, *De Monarchiâ*. It rests on the fundamental conception that the
world, being a thought of God, is designed for unity, the
attainment of which is the chief aim of man. The human
race never achieved political unity and peace except during
the reign of the Emperor Augustus, at the time of the birth
and life on earth of Jesus Christ. Various episodes of that
life (even the trial by Pontius Pilate) are cited as proofs
of His recognition of the Roman Empire. Further, the whole
history of that Empire showed it to be the organism divinely
ordained for promoting unity and peace: "The Roman
people was ordained by nature to command." There must

[1] Dante, *Purgatorio*, Canto VI, ll. 76 *et seq.*

be one such people; and Rome by her spirit, no less than by her exploits, proclaimed herself to be the executant of the divine will: "Who is so dull of mind as not by this time to see that by right of ordeal the glorious people gained for itself the crown of the whole world?"[1] What, then, has of late lost them the crown? Mainly, the conflict between Pope and Emperor. The striving of the Pope for temporal power has brought endless strife on the people which ought to be one at heart: "O blessed people! (Dante exclaims[2]) O glorious Ausonia, if only he who enfeebled thy Empire had either ne'er been born, or ne'er been misled by his own pious purpose." This vigorous outburst is directed against Constantine, whose alleged donation of the Roman domains to the Papacy was claimed as the basis of the Temporal Power of that institution.

Thus Dante, good son of the Church though he was, recognized her Temporal Power to be an evil, because it introduced strife where there ought to be harmony. Let the Pope be solely the vicar of Christ; let the Emperor wield the sword in the name of Christ. In no sense does the Emperor derive his authority from the Pope.[3] Each derives his authority from Christ: the Pope, in order to lead men to eternal life; the Emperor, to lead them to temporal felicity.

By this teaching Dante hoped to heal the strifes which desolated Italy and Germany. The conflicting authorities of Pope and Emperor were to merge; then the Roman people would once more direct human affairs. The conception is no less imaginative than statesmanlike. Pope and Emperor (i. e. in the main, Italy and Germany) were to work together for the welfare of mankind; but the guiding impulse must come from Rome, the divinely created source of religion, statesmanship, and armed might.

[1] Dante, *De Monarchiâ*, Bk. II, chs. 7, 11.
[2] Bk. II *ad fin.*   [3] Bk. III, *passim.*

In pursuance of this theme Dante sought to revive the Holy Roman Empire, Christianizing its spirit, but keeping the initiative always with "the holy Roman people." In this sense, and this alone, is Dante an Italian nationalist. To me it seems that Mazzini in his essay "On the minor Works of Dante" read into the *De Monarchiâ* much of his own perfervid nationalism. But it is true that Dante's world-empire was to be Roman. Other peoples were to yield up their wills and act in conformity with the fiat of the Eternal City. This doctrine is not Italian nationalism, very far from it. It is a flash of the old Roman Imperialism focussed in a Christian lens. But here we find the source of the inextinguishable faith in Rome which nerved many Italian patriots, even when, like Mazzini, they rejected Roman clericalism.

Dante, by ascribing a divine mission to the Roman people, exerted on the fourteenth century an influence not unlike that of the patriotic priest, Gioberti, on the mid-nineteenth century. Each declared the Romans and their descendants to be a chosen people, marked out by special gifts and consecrated by divine decree. When people believe that, they can never be wholly enslaved. They have taken the first difficult step which leads, it may be through ages of torture and despair, towards political independence. In this sense Dante was the father of Italian nationalism.

In one other respect Dante uplifted his people to an incalculable extent. He taught them to wing their thoughts to the highest ecstasies in their mother-tongue. He deliberately chose to body forth the holiest and most thrilling thoughts in the vernacular. Leaving other scholars to stalk on Latin stilts, he strode forth easily but majestically, using the language of the streets of Florence. He defended his choice in the work *De Vulgari Eloquentiâ*, which is the first conscious effort at nationalizing literature.

Other poets, notably Fazio degli Uberti (*circa* 1370), wrote canzoni more directly inspired by the national idea. But the instinct of the Italian people singles out Dante as the source of the Italian spirit. In the year 1844 Mazzini thus wrote of the mediæval seer:—

"The splendor of no other genius has been able to eclipse or dim the grandeur of Dante; never has there been a darkness so profound that it could conceal this star of promise from Italian eyes. . . . As if there had been a compact, an interchange of secret life between the nation and its poet, even the common people, who cannot read, know and revere his sacred name. The mountaineers of Tolmino, near Udine, tell the travellers that there is the grotto where Dante wrote—there the stone upon which he used to sit; yet a little while, and the country will inscribe on the base of his statue—'The Italian nation to the memory of its Prophet.'"

Yes: Italy has become a nation, and she owes her nationhood no less to the thrilling words of her seers than to the bravery of her soldiers. As will appear in the sequel, her union is due very largely to the thrilling thoughts of her gifted sons. Indeed, the unique interest attaching to the Italian movement is due to the inspiration which it drew from the noblest natures and thence spread through the masses. Italian nationality is no mechanical product, the result of warlike pressure from without, as was elsewhere often the case. It is rather a soul-politic than a body-politic.

But if the genius of Dante inspired the leaders of thought in Italy, he did not and could not inaugurate a truly national feeling. The times were not ripe for that. Lawgivers, statesmen, warriors, even inventors and mechanics, had to play their several parts before the common people in remote provinces could come into touch and feel the consciousness of a common life. As a rule, such an awakening is due to forces that compel a people to fall back on its reserves of strength;

and these forces act most potently in time of war. It is probable that Italy and Germany would have arrayed themselves in conscious hostility but for the cross currents that swept across them, diverting their fortunes into side channels and many confusing eddies.

As it was, the national issue was first definitely posed between the Western peoples. Of these the Spaniards were almost wholly immersed in the internecine struggle with the Moors, from the long agony of which there emerged the fierce ballads of the Cid as a promise of many a deed of fanatical heroism in the more prosperous future. But France and England learnt to know themselves during the earliest of the great national struggles, the Hundred Years' War. The combatants were well matched. What England lacked in bulk she made up in the excellent organization of the monarchy bequeathed by William I and Henry II to the three Edwards. The French, superior in numbers, were weakened by feudal divisions and the strifes of the great nobles. Neither State, however, was much distracted by papal or other external claims; and thus a dispute arising out of Plantagenet ambition developed into a trial of strength between two warlike peoples.

To trace in detail the growth of English and French national feeling during the course of this long struggle is an impossible task. Limiting ourselves for the present to the islanders, we may note that the loss of Normandy, unity of law and administration, and the influence of firm government under Henry II and Edward I, had prepared the way for a union of hearts between Norman and Saxon; but that union was cemented on the fields of Crecy and Poitiers. Fighting side by side against great odds, Norman knight and Saxon archer forgot their old feuds and merged their racial differences in the pride of Englishry. Thenceforth signs abound of the victorious sweep of the new insular sentiment. In 1362

proceedings in the Law Courts were ordered to be conducted
in English; and in the following year our mother-tongue
gained its Poitiers, when Edward III opened Parliament in a
speech delivered in the vernacular.

The union of Norman energy and Anglo-Saxon stubborn-
ness in a single type is an event of unique importance. For
when two or more hostile or jealous races coalesce, the result
is a notable increase of mental vigor as well as of physical
force. In England the reigns of Edward III, Elizabeth,
James I and Anne are remarkable for the broadening of
national life and also for literary triumphs which express the
fuller vitality of the time. A similar access of martial and
literary energy marks the complete union of Spain under
Ferdinand and Isabella, and that of France under Louis XIV.
These and other cases reveal the connection that exists
between politics and culture. Enlarge the outlook of peoples
previously cramped and you quicken all their faculties. The
result is frequently seen in an outburst of song, as happens
with birds at mating time. It was so in England. The age
of the Black Prince was also the age of Chaucer, Langland,
and Wycliffe. The dawn of English nationality coincided
with the dawn of a truly English literature.

There was something in the air as well as in Chaucer's
genius which prompted him to write in English. French
in ancestry, courtier by choice, and thereby condemned
to speak mainly in French, he chose to write in the tongue
of the street and mart. Moreover, not only the language,
but the spirit of his chief work is thoroughly English. In
their origin most of the "Canterbury Tales" are Italian,
or, in a few cases, French; but Chaucer's presentment is
thoroughly insular. The plot and the setting of the Tales
are aggressively Cockney or Kentish. Through Mine Host
the poet chaffs those of the company who prefer to mangle
the French language rather than speak their own. As for

the characters, they are such as might be found to-day at a village penny-reading. Perhaps it was Chaucer's captivity in France which sharpened his insular patriotism; for no experience can be more nationalizing than a time spent as prisoner of war. Whatever the cause, Chaucer was a thorough Englishman. I think that we know him as well as, and perhaps love him better than, most men of our acquaintance.

The writing of charming poems in what had before been a despised vernacular is a landmark in the national life. A people cannot attain to its full powers until its thoughts and aspirations are wedded to the mother-tongue, until that mother-tongue ceases to growl or stammer, or learns to sing. The difference in the life of the folk resembles that which comes during the growth of a youth, say, between fifteen and eighteen. The boy of fifteen is tongue-tied, awkward, perhaps a mere hobbledehoy. The youth of eighteen is a different being; he has felt the first thoughts of love; he has, perhaps, spoken them forth; he has become vocal. Possibly, too, those feelings are accompanied by others much the reverse towards an individual of his own sex. If so, he knows what jealousy or hatred is. In short, he has begun to know himself. That delicious time of life has its counterpart in the experience of a people. A crisis comes which sets the blood tingling and calls forth energies and aspirations hitherto latent. That is what happened to us at the beginning of the Hundred Years' War. The Black Prince, Chaucer, Wycliffe are the first complete manifestations of the native spirit. An indefinable energy, vigor, and splendor radiates forth from our people at that time, as it does from all peoples in the heyday of ripening manhood. So brilliant are the exploits of the Black Prince that Froissart regards England as the chosen abode of chivalry. Chaucer awakens her brain and her sense of beauty. Wycliffe speaks

to her soul. On all sides of her being the nation is awake.
It was a keen historic sense which led Shakespeare to place
in the mouth of men of that age the loftiest of patriotic
pæans. Old John of Gaunt sings his swan-song in praise of
England:—

> "This royal throne of Kings, this sceptred isle,
> This earth of majesty, this seat of Mars,
> This other Eden, demi-paradise,
> This fortress built by Nature for herself
> Against infection and the hand of war,
> This happy breed of men, this little world,
> This precious stone set in the silver sea."

And Bolingbroke, on departing for banishment:—

> "Then England's ground, farewell; sweet soil, adieu;
> My mother and my nurse, that bears me yet!
> Where'er I wander, boast of this I can,
> Though banish'd, yet a true-born Englishman." [1]

The clash of war, which first made England know herself,
also summoned to conscious life the French nation. There
again forces were at work, some promoting, others retarding,
national unity. The centripetal influences were pride in the
old Roman heritage, and the community of language and
culture which it bequeathed; also the work of the clergy,
the effects of the Crusades, and the efforts of the stronger
monarchs to promote uniformity in law and the administration. Of the centrifugal influences the chief were of
Frankish origin, the instinct to follow the chief rather than
the King, which divided the realm amongst rival and greedy
feudatories, each a law to himself and the source of law to
his vassals. The Kings, allied with the Gallic populace, were

---

[1] *Richard II*, Act I, Sc. 3; Act II, Sc. 1.

waging a doubtful conquest with the Teutonic and feudal elements, when there burst upon this divided realm the Hundred Years' War. The natural result was the triumph of the invaders, under whose blows all that was left of the French dominions began to solidify. The one possible rallying point, the monarchy, gradually gained ground over rebellious feudatories; but, owing to the contemptible weakness of Charles VII, the struggle was still going against France, when the most remarkable figure of the late Middle Ages arose to vivify her people and confound their enemies. Jeanne d'Arc left her sheep at Domrémy and came to drive forth the invaders. Her resolve to do battle against the English until Charles be crowned at Rheims was the more remarkable because legally she was not a Frenchwoman. She was born and lived in the Burgundian part of that border village. But in her meditations in the woods the high-souled maiden heard angelic voices that bade her "go into France"; and we may question whether with the religious impulse were not mingled the promptings of that national sentiment which has often spoken forth in the moving tones of a woman. The Baraks of a great crisis have rarely lacked their Deborahs; and a cause that deeply stirs woman's nature is on the road to triumph. Certain it is that the advent of Jeanne d'Arc meant infinitely much to the French; for it heartened them and bewildered their enemies; and this, not only for superstitious reasons, but also because Jeanne was France personified. No figure in history has more fully typified a nation; and when a nation sees itself thus incarnate its powers are doubled.

From our present point of view it matters little that she was captured, was deserted by the French and barbarously burnt by the English. Those actions belong to the superstition and cruelty of the time. What belongs to all time is the saintly heroic influence that radiated from her and passed into the heart of her people. While Charles VII was trimming his sails to every breeze she uttered words instinct with patriotic wisdom: "As to the peace with the English, the only one possible is that they should go back to their country in England." That is the national ideal, for the first time clearly defined. The French are one people and must possess the whole of France. There will be no peace while the islanders hold down part of France. The thought is very simple. It is the inspired common sense of a peasant girl gifted with vision. How much misery would mankind have been spared from that time to this if rulers and warriors had realized the truth, that every civilized nation, when thoroughly awakened to conscious life, must control its own destinies and will not long submit to be held down by another people.—"Let each nation be content with its natural boundaries, and not seize the lands of its equally civilized neighbors." How simple! And yet the nation which claims to be at the summit of civilization has, even now, not learnt that rudimentary lesson in the doctrine of nationality.

Notice, too, these words of Jeanne after her capture: "I know well that these English will kill me, because they hope, after my death, to gain the Kingdom of France. But, were there 100,000 more of them, they shall conquer it never, never." There spoke forth clearly for the first time the soul of France, unconquerable in the fifteenth century as in the twentieth century.

The head typifying France on the coins of the first Republic was that of a beautiful actress who became transiently famous during the Terror. Certainly, the French genius is best personified by a beautiful, high-spirited woman. But when I think of France I always see the Maid of Orleans.

Italy—not merely the Italy of to-day, but of seven centuries—seems to resolve herself into the figure of Beatrice;

or, in her many tragic phases, to be transformed into the sad yet serene features of Dante.

The English people, surely, are not well represented by the conventional Britannia. Their character, ruggedly insular yet widely adaptable, and marked by a maturity that does not age, is perhaps best typified by the genial humanism of the countenance of Chaucer or of Shakespeare.

The time is not yet ripe for limning the features of our enemies; and Russia is still somewhat of a sphinx. But that every nation has a distinct personality, who can doubt?

LECTURE II

VIVE LA NATION

"La nation, c'est vous; la loi, c'est encore vous, c'est votre volonté; le roi, c'est le gardien de la loi."—*Adresse de l'Assemblée nationale au Peuple français*, Feb. 11, 1790.

In the last lecture we found reasons for regarding Dante, Chaucer, and Jeanne d'Arc as the first exponents of the national ideal for their several peoples. But it is very doubtful whether that ideal was visible to the people at large, except in the chief crises of war. At such a time every man and woman who could think felt deep hatred of the foreign invader; and in this sense of repulsion for the foreigner nationalism of the cruder sort doubtless had its rise. Idealized though it might be by the loftier minds, yet in its lower forms it was little more than dislike of the aggressive stranger. This feeling it was which ranged French and English against one another in almost solid phalanxes.

But the cross currents, which we have noticed as confusing the issues in mediæval Germany and Italy, soon began to sweep across England and France. Both lands fell a prey to civil strifes which nearly effaced the nascent sense of unity. England, whose polity had far excelled that of other peoples, was soon distracted by religious and constitutional disputes lasting through most of the sixteenth and seventeenth centuries. In that period the Elizabethan Era stands out as a smiling oasis; for then, during a brief space, England was almost one at heart; and the Spanish menace united Englishmen of all creeds in defence of their homes and liberties. That danger past, the island realm was again rent by schisms

which the follies and perversity of the Stuarts prolonged until
the Settlement of 1688.   Consequently, English patriotism
did not fully emerge until the times of Marlborough and the
two Pitts.

The fortunes of the French were not very dissimilar.
After monarchy brought them within sight of political union
there fell on them the Wars of Religion. The exhaustion of
the people and the statecraft of Richelieu and Mazarin
finally brought about internal peace, but at the expense of
popular liberties; and the reigns of Louis XIII and XIV,
which consummated the external union of the French provinces, left the people themselves unfree and exhausted. This
state of things (not unlike that of the English under Henry
VIII) is unfavorable to the growth of patriotism, a virtue
whose highest manifestation needs a large measure of civic
freedom and an abounding vitality. The French provinces, brought together by Louis XIV, resembled a new
plantation of shrubs in time of drought. They were sapless;
their leaves drooped; they were starved by the royal oak
hard by. "L'Etat, c'est moi," exclaimed the monarch; and
it was true during his reign, when patriotism centred in the
person of the King. A political catechism, drawn up for the
training of his grandson, the Duke of Burgundy, stated that
the King represented the entire nation, which had no cor-
porate existence apart from him.[1] That was correct. During
the long interregnum of the States General (1614–1789)
the only bond of union was the royal administration; and the
edicts of the Royal Council of Ministers formed at best only a
partial protection against feudal injustice and provincial
inequalities. The people cried out for efficient government,
which could come only with a close and effective union of all
classes and provinces. Their cry finds expression in many of

[1] "La nation ne fait pas corps en France; elle réside tout entière dans
la personne du roi."

the *cahiers*, or writs of grievances, drawn up in the spring of
1789. The Commons of Beauvais demand—"an invariable
rule in all parts of the public administration and public order,
that is to say, a constitution. . . . It is because France has
never had one that her administration has been subject to
ceaseless changes and she herself has been in danger." So
again a village near Metz writes: "May all your subjects,
Sire, be made truly French by the Government, as they
already are by the love which they feel for their King."
Again: "Your peoples seek refuge at the foot of your throne
and come to seek in you their tutelary deity." [1]

These and many other similar assertions prove that France
had no constitution (though Burke denied it) and that she
fervently desired to achieve in the sphere of law and administration the national unity of which she was by this time conscious. That Louis XVI should make her effectively a nation
was at first the desire of all; and even when he egregiously
failed, and the National Assembly seized the reins from his
nerveless hands, the old instinct of regarding the King as the
keystone of the national arch for a long time survived. At
the news of his flight towards the eastern frontier at mid-
summer, 1791, the dismay of very many Frenchmen almost
resembled that which fell on the Peruvians when Pizarro and
his handful of desperadoes seized the sacred person of the
Inca. Such were the feelings of an official in a French village,
who, on learning that Louis XVI had fled, exclaimed to a
better educated acquaintance: "Alas! What shall we do?
The King has escaped." The nascent consciousness of the
new age flashed forth in the reply: "Well! If the King has
escaped, the nation remains. Let us consider what to do."
France did consider; and, after a time of compromise and
hesitation, she decided that the only thing to do with a King

[1] *Archives parlementaires*, III, 299; VI, 24, 318. See too Sorel, *L'Europe
et la Révolution française*, I, p. 187.

who desired to run away was to dethrone him. Thereafter
the idea of the nation was paramount; and, despite the
triumph of reaction in and after 1815, it has been paramount
ever since.

The delay of the French in abolishing the old monarchy
is somewhat surprising, if we remember the ardor with
which their leading thinkers had adopted the political theories
of Rousseau. The reader who peruses his chief work, *Le
Contrat Social* (1762), may not at first perceive the importance
of the national idea. But that idea is fundamental to his
whole treatise. The dominant notion of the work is of a
contract or compact by which men, when emerging from
savagery, form themselves into a civil society. Rousseau,
with the eye of faith, beholds them frame an agreement as
free men and equals; and by this mystic contract, which may
or may not have actually happened, they become citizens and
form a State. It matters not (says Rousseau) that the existence of the social contract cannot be proved. He takes it for
granted, and so do all his followers.

Now, this explanation of the rise of civil society, though
it is altogether fanciful, has exercised a potent influence.
It lies at the root of the early Socialism; and it also helped
on the national idea. Take this statement of Rousseau:
"Before examining the act by which a nation elects a King,
it would be fitting to examine the act by which a nation becomes a nation." [1] That act is the social contract, which he
then examines. When the union takes place, the result is a
body politic, a *respublica*. Men who before were separate
units are now citizens. He terms their association in its
passive aspect a State (a use of the term which is open to
grave objections). But he applies the term "sovereign" to
the body politic when it is active. Thus, according to
him, the whole body of citizens, when at rest, forms the

[1] *Contrat social*, Bk. I, ch. 5.

State;[1] when it makes laws it is "the sovereign." For purposes of convenience or efficiency it may choose a man from one family to become ruler; but his powers always remain subordinate to the real sovereign, the people.[2]

Again, when they have decided on a law or any course of action, their will is final. The "general will," as he calls it, is the ultimate court of appeal. He declares it to be inalienable, indivisible, impeccable. Before this quintessence of negations all other authority, especially that of the Church and of privileged Orders, must bow down, so that there may be no divisions in the body politic. It must be compact in order to be supreme; and that supremacy must have no limits. The newly formed nation may make use of a legislator to draw up laws; but even then its authority is dominant.

Now, in this sweeping claim we have the foundation, not only of modern democracy, but also of nationality in a complete and conscious sense. The influence exerted by Rousseau on the development of the national idea has not, I think, been sufficiently emphasized. Every student knows that *Le Contrat Social* is the source of French democratic notions; but that work is equally the fountainhead of modern nationalism. Before Rousseau, writers on government and law had been comparatively little influenced by the idea of the nation. Montesquieu, writing only some fourteen years before Rousseau, scarcely mentions the nation. He sometimes seems to feel his way towards that idea as influencing the character of laws; but only in that particular. It was reserved for Rousseau to set forth the national idea with a force and cogency which opened up a new era both in thought and deed.

[1] Again, Bk. II, ch. 10: "It is the men that constitute the State."
[2] Dante, in the *De Monarchiâ*, proclaimed this truth: "For citizens do not exist for the Consuls, nor the nation for the King; but, on the contrary, the Consuls for the citizens, the King for the nation."

The Swiss thinker not only gave birth to the idea of the nation, but he endowed it with the strength of an infant Hercules. The French people could scarcely have achieved the miracles of the new age had they not been doubly inspired. The notion of liberty, doubtless, was the chief impulse urging them forward; but with it there then worked the powerful feeling of nationality. For the first time in their history all Frenchmen realized their essential oneness. That is a unique occasion in the life of a people. We know what it meant from our experience in August, 1914. Then, for the first time in our history, the peoples of the whole of the British Empire were enthusiastically of one mind; and the mighty unison was not marred, only emphasized, by a few thin discordant pipings. Much the same was it in the France of 1789. Resolute in her quest for liberty, she was nerved by the consciousness that practically all her children were one at heart. From the cramped sphere of provincialism they rose by one bound to the far loftier plateau of nationality. There they breathed the pure air of freedom and were exhilarated by contact with others whom they had deemed half foreigners and now found to be Frenchmen. The results of this double inspiration were portentous. Relatively to the still torpid peoples of the Continent, the Frenchman of the Revolution was a superman.

After that brief time of exhilaration, which inspired Wordsworth and Coleridge with some of their best work, the then allied ideas of liberty and nationality were destined soon to come into collision, with results disastrous to the cause of progress. We who are living amidst a cataclysm such as the world has never known can realize the extent of the disaster; and we find it difficult to understand the buoyancy of heart, the vigor in action, of the year 1789, when the two powerful principles, Liberty and Nationality, pulled together. Then the human race experienced the spring tide of achievement.

May it be the lot of us, who now toil through the dead time of the neap tides, to be borne ahead once again on that bounding flood!

The dominance of the national idea in the early part of the French Revolution is obvious at many points. Very significant is the title assumed by the Tiers État (Commons) of the States General. That body, hitherto divided into three distinct Orders, had not met during 175 years: and the Commons desired to break with the past. After long deliberations as to various cumbrous titles that had been proposed, an obscure member called out: "*Assemblée nationale.*" "Yes, yes," they all cried; and the motion was carried, despite the grave fears of Mirabeau and others, who foresaw its destructive effect on the monarchy. The name, indeed, recalled the ambitious claim of Sieyès in his pamphlet *Qu'est-ce que le Tiers État,* that the Commons formed the nation; the Commons (said he) furnish all the productive classes, from professors to lacqueys; therefore they are the nation. This term he defined thus: "a body of associates living under a common law and represented by a single legislature." The definition is utterly defective because mechanical; it would include such cases as the peoples of the old Holy Roman Empire, or of the Indian Empire of to-day where there is no real unity of sentiment. But this cold, mechanical definition inspirited the deputies of France to seek for a single legislature; and so what had been merely the unprivileged Order of the ancient States General became the National Assembly, the organ of the general will (June 17, 1789). In vain did Louis XVI seek to force the deputies back into the three distinct Orders. In vain did he declare that if they could not agree, he alone would effect the welfare of his *peoples.* He spoke the language of the past. No longer were they diverse peoples sheltered by his care. The thinking part of France now realized that the nation existed apart from him. Such, too, was the significance of the famous Tennis Court Oath of June 20, when the deputies, without a single reference to the King, swore never to part until they had made a constitution.

The consequences of this change of outlook were momentous. Even in the first and very moderate draft of the Rights of Man, which Mounier presented to the National Assembly on July 27, there is this significant clause: "The principle of complete sovereignty resides essentially in the nation. No corporation, no individual, can exercise authority which does not emanate expressly from it."

The essence of the Revolution lies in those words. They enthrone the nation and dethrone the King of France. Thenceforth he becomes "the hereditary representative," as he is often termed; while all public bodies are subjected to the nation. The Roman Catholic Church is forced to acknowledge the supremacy of the State; and the abolition of all bodies, like the old Parlements, which contest that supremacy, is a foregone conclusion. With the Parlements vanish the Provinces and all their local exemptions and rights. From Brittany to Provence, from French Flanders to Spanish Roussillon, there is a clean sweep of all the local privileges which had fettered the action of the old monarchy; and in the spring of 1790 France stood forth united, unshackled, as she never had been. Against myriads of local or social abuses which had defied the absolute monarchy, the nation forthwith prevailed. Some of its early champions sought to moderate its zeal. Among them, Mounier endeavored to arouse the local feeling of Dauphiné, where he and the provincial Estates had exercised a paramount influence. But now throughout France there was but one cry: "We are not provincials; we are Frenchmen"; and before the cry "Vive la Nation" down went all the walls of privilege and local custom.

The resistance which Mounier offered in Dauphiné served

to inaugurate those federations of towns and villages which
helped on the levelling process. The first of these unions of
citizens with those of neighboring towns took place at
Étoile on the Rhone, in Dauphiné, in November, 1789. There
the townsfolk and peasants assembled, some 12,000 strong,
fully armed as National Guards, and took the following oath:
"We, soldier-citizens of both banks of the Rhone, fraternally
assembled for the public welfare, swear before high heaven,
on our hearts and on our weapons devoted to the defence of
the State, that we will remain for ever united. Abjuring every
distinction of our provinces [Languedoc and Dauphiné],
offering our arms and our wealth to the fatherland, for the
support of the laws which come from the National Assembly,
we swear to give all possible succor to each other to fulfil
these sacred duties, and to fly to the help of our brothers of
Paris, or of any town of France which may be in danger, in
the cause of liberty." [1] This episode is of high significance.
It sounded forth the call to national unity on behalf of the
peasants and small traders; and, throughout the next eight
months, similar federations of districts or Departments
helped to abolish provincialism. The climax was reached in
the national Festival of Federation, held in the Champ de
Mars on July 14, 1790. A spectator, the denationalized
German baron, "Anacharsis" Clootz, pointed the moral of
the episode by a reference to the mass meetings of Celtic and
Frankish warriors yearly held on that spot: "It carries you
back two thousand years by an indefinable tone of antiquity:
it carries you forward two thousand years by the rapid
progress of reason, of which this federation is the precocious
and delectable foretaste." Certainly these federations helped
to brand on the French the feeling of indissoluble oneness. It
is easy to pass a law for political union; it is a far more difficult
thing to secure a union of hearts. Our Union with Ireland in

[1] *Hist. parlementaire*, IV, p. 3.

1801 is an example of the former; the French Departmental System of 1790 achieved the latter, because the people themselves at once registered the edict of their legislators. Thenceforth Celtic Brittany, the half-Flemish north, the half-Spanish Roussillon, and almost wholly German Alsace threw in their lot for ever with France.

Yes, for ever. This present war is in part the outcome of this resolve of Alsace and North-east Lorraine to be French, not German. Whether Germany might not have won over the Alsacians if her treatment had been less brutal is an open question. But the outcome is that Alsace has never been Germanized, and that a province, which is almost entirely Teutonic by race, is still almost entirely French at heart. It was the magical influence of the great idea incarnate in the France of the Revolution which won that heart for the French nation.

One of the distinctive features of those federations of 1790 was the exaltation of law. It is rather difficult in England to imagine rustics and small shopkeepers assembling in tens of thousands for the glorification of law. Generally, when they assemble in large numbers it is for the opposite purpose. But, when one remembers that in France the old feudal and royal edicts had been the detested decrees of a class or of a domain, one can see why the populace hailed the dawn of a régime of truly national law. For by 1790 law was the same for all classes. It had swept away the distinctive Orders. It had abolished the old game laws, corvées, gabelles, and other means of oppression; and recently it had mapped out France in Departments and smaller self-governing areas, with nearly 4,300,000 "active" citizens, to whom fell the duty of electing all the officials. Thus, law had become what Rousseau had declared it ought to be, the expression of the general will. Therefore it occupied a place in the new political trinity. "The Nation, the King, the Law," such were the sacred entities in the new Order.—The Nation, the source of all political energy; the King, merely its first officer; the Law, its channel.

Every feeling that makes the heart of man beat high conspired to make those federations scenes of inspiration and strength. They were the social contracts of the young democracy. Imagine in the square of the town or village an altar of green sods erected to *la patrie;* the patriarch of the village, or else the curé, administers the patriotic oath; children dressed in white are taught what it means; and the day ends in dances and merry-making. At one village in the Cevennes, where religious passions previously ran high, the curé and the Protestant pastor meet and embrace at the national altar; then the Roman Catholics conduct the Protestants to church and listen to the pastor's address; next the Protestants conduct the others to their church and hear the words of the curé.

On other federative groups there descended the genius of patriotic doggerel. We read of one occasion when the curé composed verses on the spot and also chanted a Hymn to Liberty; whereupon the mayor felt moved to reply in stanzas, the purport of which was undiscoverable. Worthy folk! You typify French patriotism at its loftiest pitch. Did fate permit you to see the ghastly sequel?

In view of all the scenes that followed, it is not surprising that Thomas Carlyle poured a douche of his cold northern sarcasm on all that southern demonstrativeness. But, after all, were those federation festivals merely "mighty fireworks" or a "grand theatricality"? Surely they were something far deeper than that. The sensitive, impressionable Gauls need to visualize their political creed; and they hold it all the more strongly for having exulted about it.

The strength of the national instinct appeared in grim guise when war broke out between France and the German

Powers. The causes of that war do not concern us here.
What concerns us is that it was a measuring of strength
between an armed nation on the one side and two artificial
though well-disciplined States on the other. The French
Revolutionists had no doubt as to the issue. Ill-armed and
drilled though they were, they believed in their power to
overcome the professional armies drilled in the school of
Eugène and Frederick. Brissot, the bellicose wire-puller of
the Girondin group, desired to disguise some French soldiers
near the frontier as Austrians to sack and burn French villages in order to hurry on the rupture; and on a far higher
plane, Vergniaud, the great Girondin orator, appealed to
the National Assembly to commence a crusade which would
liberate other peoples still unfree. Even so moderate a
thinker as the Swiss publicist, Mallet du Pan, prophesied
in the *Mercure de France*, in January, 1792, that Austria
and Prussia would be defeated unless they could emblazon
on their banners the device, "the Charter of the Nations";
for that alone could fitly oppose the watchword on the lips
of the hosts of France, "The Rights of Man." [1] Of course,
the German Powers did not adopt Mallet's advice. Brunswick's manifesto, issued at Coblentz in deference to the
émigrés, laid stress on the restoration of royalty in France and
the punishment of all rebels.

This was the first of the many blunders of the German
Allies in 1792-3. From the outset they exasperated French
national feeling, when their aim should have been to separate
the moderates from the extreme Jacobins then in power at
Paris. They ruined the French monarchy which they came
to rescue; for they identified the cause of royalty with that
of the invaders who were coming to partition France.

After the fall of the French monarchy, in August, 1792,
the national idea acquired a force never known before. Pre-

[1] Mallet du Pan, *Mems.*, I, 249.

viously it had been confused by the lingering sense of devotion to the King and Queen. But, after the overthrow of the monarchy the issue was clear. French democracy and nationality were ranged against the German invaders and royalism; and the French were compelled to put forth all their strength and energy. In August and September, 1792, they had practically no Government; the exchequer was empty; credit had vanished; and the armies were for a time leaderless. But it is in such straits that patriotism becomes a burning force that shrivels up quibbling factions and kindles boundless energy. Only when a nation is stripped of all external aids and is faced with absolute ruin does it discover its reserves of strength. If they are utilized in time it may encounter defeats, but it will not perish. The spirit which then nerved France is finely expressed in the appeal of the young poet, André Chénier: "All ye who have a fatherland and know what it means; ye for whom the words 'to live free or die' mean something; ye who have wives, children, parents, friends for whom ye would conquer or die—how long shall we speak of our liberty? . . . Come forth. Let the nation appear."

It did appear—an armed nation. Service in the National Guards had, from the beginning of the Revolution, been one of the recognized duties of citizenship. No definite decree declared it to be either universal or compulsory; but the Constitution of 1791 laid it down that all "active citizens" were National Guards. The National Guards were merely citizens called to uphold the force of the State. For the present they did not form an organized force.[1] They therefore held a rather indefinite position. In principle every citizen was a soldier; only he was not drilled. Probably this vague state of things resulted from the conflict of opinion which had broken out in the National Assembly

[1] *Constitution of* 1791, ch. V, § 4.

during the debates of December, 1789, on military service. Dubois Crancé, a strong democrat, insisted on universal service: "I tell you that in a nation which desires to be free, which is surrounded by powerful neighbors and harassed by factions, every citizen ought to be a soldier, and every soldier a citizen, if France is not to be utterly annihilated. . . . How is it possible to make a man march forth to battle whose indolence has driven him into the ranks . . . who in fact has sold his liberty for a price, side by side with the man who has taken up arms to defend liberty? . . . It is necessary to establish a truly national conscription, which should include every one from the second man in the Kingdom down to the last active citizen." The Duc de Liancourt, Mirabeau, and others resisted this proposal as contrary to the principles of liberty and of the Rights of Man, besides being prejudicial to a complex industrial society; and the Assembly decided in favor of voluntary enlistment for the regular army; but it did not impose any rule respecting the National Guards.[1]

When war seemed imminent in the early part of 1792 many thousands of National Guards volunteered for service at the front to fill up the gaps in the regular army caused by desertion. Consequently the armed forces of France were in a chaotic state at the beginning of the war with the German Powers. Great efforts were made in July, 1792, to attract more volunteers. The alarm gun on the Pont Neuf was fired once an hour. Bands paraded the streets. Speeches were delivered at the recruiting tents; and thousands of patriotic youths at once enlisted. If we may credit the very critical estimate of von Sybel, these efforts produced little result. He says that only 60,000 recruits were forthcoming

---

[1] Jung, *Dubois-Crancé*, I, pp. 16–28, quoted by Morse Stephens, *French Rev.*, I, 383; *Procès Verbaux de l'Assemblée Nationale*, IX, X, Dec. 12 and 16.

between July 11 and September 20. It is also well known that the French success at Valmy was decided by the steadiness of the troops of the old royal army, and still more by the timidity of the Duke of Brunswick, who never pressed home his attack.

All this may be granted; and the admissions somewhat dim the glamor of those days. Yet it is undeniable that the enthusiasm which the volunteers brought to the front was a weighty factor in determining the issue on the hill of Valmy. All the life and energy were on the side of the French. Experience and mechanical discipline were ranged under the banners of Prussia; and in the few moments when the issue seemed doubtful the mighty shout of "Vive la Nation" rooted the French to the earth and carried doubt and dismay to the hearts of the invaders. Well might Goethe, who was present at the German headquarters, declare that that day inaugurated a new epoch in the history of the world. That was true. It inaugurated the era of militant democracy.

Subsequent events served to dull democracy and quicken militancy. The contrast between the political chaos at Paris and the conquering march of the French into Holland, Germany, and Italy was so sharp as to become a grave danger to an impressionable people. Unable to achieve political liberty at home, they overpowered all opposition abroad; and thus the very men who had hailed the war of 1792 as a crusade on behalf of the liberty of enslaved peoples were soon drawn into methods inconsistent with their political principles. In the constitution of 1791 they declared solemnly that the French nation would never undertake a war for the sake of making conquests. Yet the constitution of 1795 declared that all lands up to the Rhine and the Alps were thenceforth an integral part of France. This solemn declaration, that France intended to fight on until she gained her "natural limits," was an event of sinister import, preluding two decades of war; for Waterloo was the final retort to the French claim for the Rhine and Alps.

How are we to explain that extravagant claim? In part, of course, by that luckless statement of Cæsar that those were the boundaries of Gaul. But the new Gospel of Nature here reinforced the old Cæsarism. Rousseau in his essay, "A Treaty of Perpetual Peace," urged that natural features, such as mountains and rivers, seemed to mark out the bounds of the nations of Europe; and (he added) "one may say that the political order of this part of the world is in certain respects the work of nature." This incautious utterance of the master, which subordinated men's feelings to the lie of the land, was exceedingly useful to his followers. In November, 1792, when the French desired to annex Savoy, Bishop Grégoire, in his report on that topic, made use of similar arguments. As a certain number of Savoyards petitioned for union with France, he insisted that this was their universal desire; and he then stated that "the order of Nature would be contravened if their Government was not identical [with ours]." The turn of the Belgians came next, early in 1793. As for the Germans of the Rhineland, they were not consulted at all. And thus it came about that the national impulse in France, which up to 1791 promised to link all free peoples in a friendly federation, soon degenerated into a warlike and aggressive impulse, the parent of rapine abroad and of Cæsarism in France herself.

LECTURE III

SCHILLER AND FICHTE

"The first original and truly natural frontiers of States are un-questionably their spiritual frontiers."—FICHTE, *Addresses to the German Nation*, No. XII.

IT is difficult now to realize the divisions and helplessness of Germany in the eighteenth and early nineteenth centuries. Split up into some three hundred different domains, for which the Holy Roman Empire provided no effective bond of union; distracted, too, by the endless rivalry of the chief States, Austria and Prussia, the Germans seemed doomed to subservience to their better organized neighbors. The energizing and new grouping of these torpid fragments was the greatest political event of the nineteenth century.

Before its commencement, there was no desire for close union on a national basis. The ideals of the leaders of German thought were international. Very characteristic are the words penned by the philosopher Kant, at Königsberg, in his tractate, *Perpetual Peace*, 1795. "If Fortune ordains that a powerful and enlightened people should form a Republic—which by its very nature is inclined to perpetual peace—this would serve as a centre of federal union for other States wishing to join, and thus secure conditions of freedom among the States in accordance with the idea of the law of nations."

In that passage Kant expressed the aspirations of his age for a federative and pacific union of nations. The idea had been cherished in France among the more reasonable of the Girondins, and found expression in the hope that neighbor-

34

ing States would form Republics which would link on to France and gradually extend the bounds of liberty. The German thinker warmly adopted this programme and included it among the conditions conducive to the abolition of war. If it had come about, the world would have taken a long stride forward towards the international ideal. In that case France would have passed quickly through the national phase, impelled onwards towards a far loftier ideal, that of ministering to the needs of humanity at large. The years 1791-2 formed, perhaps, the most favorable opportunity in that direction that the world has ever known. For at that time Europe was in a transition stage. With the exception of England and France, the peoples had not yet awakened to full political consciousness. True, they had thrilled at the news of the French Revolution; but the first message that it sent forth from Paris was international. The motto—"Liberty, Equality, Fraternity"—was for all peoples on equal terms; and all seemed likely to press forward to the goal, without the jostling which Nationalism soon engendered. In 1792-4 there was a chance that the Germans of the Rhineland would accept the French connection, if it were really fraternal and not too paternal. At first the German reformers fraternized with the French troops. That eminent *savant*, Forster of Mainz, went up to some French National Guards then in garrison in his city, and exclaimed—"Long live the Republic!" to which there came the discouraging reply, "She will live very well without you."

The incident is characteristic of the superiority then affected by the French over the divided and benighted Germans. That feeling had long permeated the Parisian factions that desired a war of propaganda. So far back as October, 1791, the first leader of the Girondins, that restless wire-puller, Brissot, had attacked the German Powers in the most provocative terms, and his colleague, Isnard, fired off the following salvos on November 29: "A people in a state of revolution is invincible. . . . Let us tell Europe that, if the Cabinets engage the Kings in a war against the peoples, we will engage the peoples in a war against the Kings"—this, too, at a time when the Austrian and Prussian monarchs had withdrawn their former veiled threats of intervention, to which, indeed, they had scant means of giving effect.   Central and Southern Europe were so wretchedly weak that the foremost publicist of the time, Mallet du Pan, wrote thus of the chances of a successful attack by France: "Divided into a multitude of separate governments, Europe offers few bases for a common resistance, and the first great nation which changes the face of society has to fear only dissociated units." [1]

The words are a remarkable forecast of the collapse of the old order before the new; and the sequel was to show the peril that besets wars of propaganda.   Lofty though the motives of the crusaders may be at the outset, they are apt speedily to degenerate under the lure of conquest.   A strong nation which overruns weak States will in the process reveal the truth of the farseeing remark of Montesquieu, that, if a Republic subdues other peoples, its own liberty is endangered by the authority which it entrusts to its generals and proconsuls.   In the campaigns of 1793-9 France triumphed too easily.   Her profoundly national system too speedily upset the European equilibrium; and in the process the liberator merged into the mere conqueror.   The results were soon felt by the "liberated" Germans of the Rhineland.   The fraternal embracings of the first few days soon gave place to exactions, confiscations, forced loans, even to plunder.   The irreligious customs of the French troops completed the work of disillusionment; and when those harpies, the military contractors, flew on the spoil, the Germans

[1] Mallet du Pan, *Méms.*, I, 251.

experienced all the miseries of the conquered. All the salaried posts in the new administration were given to French officials, often of a very corrupt type. The soldiery bettered their example, until, in 1799, a Rhinelander complained that everybody concealed money and valuables in order to save something from the orgies of plunder. In the five years after the French occupation of 1794–5 exactions amounting to £6,000,000 were wrung from the Rhineland; and there was a general regret for the earlier time of undisturbed slumber under equally somnolent translucencies and abbesses.

The change of tone in German literature between 1789 and 1799 is remarkable. In August, 1789, the Swabian poet, Schubart, had extolled the felicity of the Germans in Alsace, who shared in the blessings of the French Revolution, while behind them (i. e. in Germany) cracked the whip of the despot. But, after the French conquest of the Rhineland, references to France and to her Revolution become cold and critical. In the writings of Goethe there are comparatively few references to the public sentiment of the time; for, as he explained in *Wahrheit und Dichtung* (anno 1775), "Our object was to get to know man; we were content to let people in general go their own way." This aloofness from the aims and strivings of the masses is a noteworthy feature of Goethe's character. It probably explains his indifference to the struggles of his countrymen against Napoleon, which sometimes has been ascribed to want of patriotism. That charge is unjust; for there are persons so constituted as to be unable to take interest in the collective activities of mankind. In their eyes the soul of man is the only study of any worth. The strivings of the many weary or disgust them. They are interested in the problems of the individual life; but popular movements, whether present or past, leave them cold. Such was the cast of Browning's mind. Though he lived in the midst of the most romantic of national movements, that of Italy, he has left no poem inspired by it; whereas Mrs. Browning, who possessed the collective sense, has left many such poems. Goethe, like Browning, lacked that sympathy with the masses, which every ardent reformer and patriot must possess. Such minds do not vibrate responsive to the appeal of the many in the present, or to that appeal from the past, which is the very soul of history.

In Goethe's writings, as in those of Browning, there are only scattered references to public affairs. But in *Hermann und Dorothea* (1797) there is this passage: "The man who, in a tottering age, is unsteady in character only increases the evil and spreads it further and further. . . . It is not for the Germans to carry on the terrible Revolution, and to waver hither and thither." The words show that Goethe, for all his cosmopolitan leanings, cherished little hope for liberation by France. In his opinion the revolutionary movement had gone astray; and mankind could hope for improvement only by the steady development of all that was best in the leading nations.

The disillusionment comes out most clearly in the works of Schiller. His sensitive spirit thrilled responsive to the collective impulses of his time. Indeed, his works form a mirror of the age. His first play, *The Robbers* (1779), produced in his twentieth year, belongs to the poetry of revolt. Animated by his defiance of law and custom, all spirited German students then dreamt of overthrowing the petty tyrannies around them—a topic portrayed in *The Robbers* with school-boy extravagance. Later on, when for a time he quitted the drama for the domain of history, his thoughts still turned towards topics of rebellion. His *Revolt of the Netherlands* and *Thirty Years' War* deal with upheavals that affected many peoples. It is the downfall of tyranny, the progress of mankind in its sterner experiences, that interested

Schiller. Like Lessing and many other German thinkers of that age, he was not a national patriot; he was a cosmopolitan. Those leaders in thought and literature did not belong to Jena, Wolfenbüttel, Weimar; they belonged to the world at large; and their thoughts touched the imagination in spheres far removed from the ducal or electoral States in which they were conceived. Those writers, cramped though their surroundings were, gave to the world a literature no less universal than that of Voltaire, Diderot, and the Encyclopædists. How strange, that those giants of the eighteenth century should have prided themselves on the effacement of national boundaries at the time when the political convulsion partly brought about by their teaching was destined to parcel out the peoples in distinct and hostile groups!

As an example of Schiller's contempt for a merely national patriotism, take this fine passage from one of his letters, dealing with the aim which the historian ought to set before him. It was written in 1789, shortly after he became Professor of History at Jena:—

"This is the problem; to choose and arrange your materials, so that, in order to interest, they shall not have the need of decoration. We moderns have a source of interest at our disposal which no Greek or Roman was acquainted with, and which the *patriotic* interest does not nearly equal. This last, in general, is chiefly of importance for unripe nations, for the youth of the world. But we may excite a very different sort of interest if we represent each remarkable occurrence that happened to *men* as being of importance to *man*. It is a poor and little aim to write for one nation; a philosophic spirit cannot tolerate such limits, cannot bound its views to a form of human nature so arbitrary, fluctuating, accidental. The most powerful nation is but a fragment; and thinking minds will not grow warm on its account, except in so far as this nation or its fortunes have exercised influence on the progress of the species."

"Arbitrary, fluctuating, accidental"; these terms well describe the life of the average German State—a mere atom in a kaleidoscope. How could one feel much enthusiasm about Würtemberg, Anhalt, or the little county of Limburg-Styrum, with its standing army of six officers and two privates! Yet it was in some of those pigmy societies that the human mind took its loftiest flights; and it is open to question whether small States, the life of which is homely and the burdens light, do not favor the growth of the intellect far better than the enormous aggregations of the present, with their vast and diffuse aims, their complex problems, and the crushing load of taxation and military service. Contrast the cast-iron philosophy and brassy literature of modern Germany with that of the quaint and kindly age which witnessed the birth every year of some masterpiece ennobling the life of the little town. Which is the greater Germany? That of Goethe or that of Wilhelm II?

A figure equally typical of the serene cosmopolitanism of old Germany is the philosopher Fichte (1762–1814). We are concerned now only with his ideas on national development; but in a later lecture I shall return to his theory of the State, which contains much that is questionable, even dangerous. Here I wish to point out the contrast between his earlier and later teachings in reference to the German polity. The most important work of his earlier period is the series of lectures entitled "Characteristics of the Present Age," which he delivered to a general audience at Berlin in 1804–5. The lectures are remarkable for their complete neglect of the principle of nationality, though revolutionary France was largely the product of that potent force. Fichte discourses at large on the human race as a whole. He asks: What is the plan of the world? What is the fundamental idea of human life viewed collectively? In Lecture I he defines it thus: "The End of the life of mankind on earth is this—that in this life they may order all their relations with freedom according to reason." [1] Stated with Anglo-Saxon bluntness, this means that Reason is to rule in human affairs, and that men ought to be free to choose the methods by which they act reasonably. Everywhere in his lectures he considers Europe as a whole. There is no need to follow him in his tedious mapping-out of the different ages of human history, except to notice his conviction, that the world was then in the third age—that of liberation from external authority. He declares the age to be one of unrestrained licence and selfishness; but he hopes that the race will ultimately win its way back to justification and sanctification. In all his tedious disquisition there is no sign that he perceives the force of national differences and of the diverse parts which different nations may have to play. With serene indifference to such distinctions, he assumes that somehow mankind will move, or be moved, onward through the five cycles. In Lecture XIV he says: "The Christian Europeans are essentially but one people; they recognize this common Europe as their one true Fatherland; and, from one end of it to the other, pursue nearly the same purposes and are ever actuated by similar motives." The statement proves how blind cosmopolitan philosophers can be to disagreeable facts. Enclosing themselves in their own theories, and confusing what is with what ought to be, minds of that order often construct a world of their own, and rail at persons who remind them of the existence of the world of actualities. Fichte, in his earlier phase, was one of these philosophizing spiders, living in a web which he had evolved from his inner consciousness, and calling it the world. Consider the facts. Napoleon had overrun Hanover and the Kingdom of Naples in the endeavor to beat down the British Power. He had turned Germany upside down with his Secularizations, and the war

[1] Fichte, *Characteristics of the Present Age* (Eng. Transl., p. 5).

was clearly about to become world-wide; for Russia and Austria were arming against the great Emperor, who recklessly defied them. Yet Fichte says that all Christian peoples recognize Europe as their common Fatherland, are pursuing nearly the same purposes, and are actuated by similar motives.

Elsewhere, however, he admits that these Christian States are striving perpetually for supremacy. Sometimes one prevails: then another; and (says Fichte) the truly enlightened man will always owe allegiance to the one which prevails—a startling touch of worldly prudence. Only the earth-born souls will remain citizens of the fallen State, recognizing their Fatherland in its soil, and rivers and mountains, which is all they desire. But "the sun-like Spirit, irresistibly attracted, will wing its way wherever there is Light and Liberty. And in this cosmopolitan frame of mind we may look with perfect serenity on the actions and the fate of Nations, for ourselves and our successors, even to the end of Time."

This theory, if translated into practice, works out thus: If Prussia prevails over Austria, all enlightened Germans will transfer their allegiance to her. If France prevails over Prussia, these neo-Prussians will become Frenchmen at heart. If France falls, and there ensues a complete Balance of Power these political chameleons will run about distracted, seeking in vain for a predominant color. Was Fichte's fluid cosmopolitanism the outcome of despair at Germany's helplessness and of Napoleon's omnipotence? Or did he share Goethe's conviction as to the need of renovation by "the new Charlemagne"? It is difficult to say. One thing alone is clear, his utter indifference to the claims of country. Whether France, Prussia, or Austria gained the supremacy was nothing to him.

No! The national idea in Germany was first set forth

by a man who dealt, not with abstractions but realities, not
with States but peoples. While Fichte was groping his way
through these hazy abstractions, a poet and historian found
his way to firm ground. Schiller gave to the world *Wilhelm
Tell* (1804).

He designed it as "a national drama, in sympathy with
all the liberal tendencies of the age." I believe that he
hoped to stir up a truly German feeling, and thus stay the
dry-rot that was creeping into the life of his people. With
the insight of a poet he had long noted the strength of patriotism. The national revival of France, effected by the
Maid of Orleans, had inspired his drama on that subject;
and in 1803–4 he turned his thoughts towards the German
Swiss of the Forest Cantons. The inner meaning of the
play lies in the conflict between the free mountaineers of the
Ur-Cantonen and the greed and usurpation of the House
of Hapsburg. True, the human interest of the story centres
in the character and action of the legendary hero, Tell.
The drama must have heroes, not heroic abstractions; and
Tell is a fine specimen of the Swiss mountaineer, frank,
generous, unsuspicious, no meddler in politics, and slow to
act against recognized authority. He is the central figure of
the drama; but he is not the moving spirit of its action. That
spirit is the instinct of the people. Outraged by the barbarities of the Hapsburg soldiery, that instinct asserts itself
at first in saving this or that defender of his home; further
than this Tell will not go. He represents the average good-
natured mountaineer, who will save an individual, but
does not understand political action, so that he is reproached
for his want of fervor in the common cause. In fact, the
instinct of the people wells forth most fully in the person
of a woman. Gertrud is the moving influence of the piece.
While her husband, Werner Stauffacher, seems likely to
endure tamely all the threats and insolence of the Hapsburg

officers, she counsels resistance; and when he speaks of the horrors of war she replies:—

"Look forward, Werner, not behind you, now."

When again he reminds her of the nameless fate that may befall her, she utters these lofty words:—

"None are so weak, but one last choice is left.
A leap from yonder bridge, and I am free."

Spurred to action by his wife's heroism, Stauffacher takes counsel with other men of Unterwalden; and they resolve to assemble on the Rütli rock above the Lake of Lucerne, meeting there the men of Schywtz and Uri. In that primeval solitude, and under cover of night, they assemble to renew the ancient bond of union between the three cantons. Acts of brutal tyranny by the minions of Austria now bring together men long sundered in times of peace. They listen as Stauffacher unfolds to them the story of their Germanic parentage; how, driven forth by famine from the northern plain, their forefathers forced a way into the Swiss mountains and made them homes in diverse valleys; yet ever were they mindful of their Switzer origin. Now, against Hapsburg usurpation they must make common cause, not only as free Switzers, but also as loyal sons of the old Germanic Empire.

Before they swear to resist Austria's novel claims, a priest, Rosselmann, steps into the ring and urges them, for the sake of peace and quietness, to give way before Austria. One and all, they scout the proposal as that of a traitor; and they pass this decree:—

"Whoe'er
Shall talk of tamely bearing Austria's yoke,
Let him be stripped of all his rights and honors;
And no man hence receive him at his hearth."

After this drastic treatment of the pacifist case, they proceed to renew their bond of union:—

> "We swear to be a nation of true brothers,
> Never to part in danger or in death."
> *(They swear, with three fingers raised.)*
> "We swear we will be free as were our sires,
> And sooner die than live in slavery."
> *(They swear, as before.)*

What is this but a Social Contract in a poetical setting? Schiller had been an enthusiastic student of Rousseau; and he believed firmly in the formation of political societies by the action of the people, which would necessarily lead to liberty and harmony. The States thus formed would be strong and stable, far different from the artificial areas ruled over by German princelings. The new Germanic State or States would guarantee the welfare of Germans and keep at arm's length the aggressor. The tone of the drama is throughout intensely German. The last scenes reveal the peasants free, united, and happy, while the House of Hapsburg is rent asunder by revolt and by the murder of its chief.

The moral of it all is clear. Schiller appeals to his countrymen to forget their miserable divisions which have left them a prey to the aggressions of Napoleon. He seems to say to the Germans of his day: "Will you not forget your absurd differences? Will you not join hands across the political barriers, and unite for the defence of your honor and your dearest interests? Only so can you save the Fatherland from subjection to an insolent usurper. Your princes cannot, or will not, save you. Your own right hands, your own good sense, must save you from servitude to the foreigner."

This, surely, is the inner meaning of the drama. It describes the birth of a nation, and as such it is regarded by

all Switzers. They look back to the scene on the Rütli rock
as the beginning of their political life. Whether that event
is historical, or semi-historical, or legendary is of small account. Even if it be legendary, it has exerted upon the
fortunes of Switzerland an influence more important than
that of cartloads of documents of unimpeachable authen-
ticity. It is one of those episodes which make the heart of a
people beat fast with pride and hope. In the Swiss House
of Parliament at Berne the Rütli scene has been painted
large on the wall behind the President's chair. In that Parliament there are men who speak French, German, and Italian;
but the feeling of unity aroused by the contemplation of that
scene transcends mere diversities of tongue, and merges the
fragments of those now warring peoples in a fervidly Swiss
nationality, which bids fair to outlast even the divulsive
influences of this war.[1] It is true that the strain just now on
Swiss nationality is very severe; and the sharp tension which
prevails between the German and the Latin portions reveals
the strength of the tie of language. But here lies the interest
of the case of Switzerland. The Swiss cherish a collective
sentiment which far transcends race and language, a sentiment springing from pride in a glorious past and love of the
mountains around which they cluster. The Swiss will, I
believe, remain a nation, and will not merge into the three
great peoples that surround them. Their keen historic sense,
their romantic attachment to their mountains and rivers,
will keep them united. In this respect they are the "earth-
born souls" at whom Fichte scoffed; and this clinging to the
soil, this pride in their achievements, will, I venture to say,
help to keep Switzerland a united whole. In this sense the

---

[1] Count Mamiani, *Rights of Nations* [Eng. edit., 1860], p. 44, says that
the Swiss are not "in the ordinary sense properly a nation." This I
deny. For, as I shall show, in Lecture VIII, it is sentiment and will,
not language, that make a nation.

legend of Wilhelm Tell, and the presentment of it by Schiller, form a national asset of priceless worth.

For Germany, too, *Wilhelm Tell* soon became preëminently the national drama. The instinct of the people caught at the truth which was there enshrined. Thenceforth Napoleon was regarded as the national enemy, and union against him as the paramount duty of all. The patriotic songs in this and others of Schiller's dramas inspired thousands of youths who went gladly into the almost hopeless struggle against the great Emperor. As was finely said at a meeting in memory of Schiller: "Thousands who trembled not when the earth groaned with the weight of the despot's mailed cavalry; men who with fearless hearts confronted the thunder of his artillery . . . all carried with them into the struggle the enthusiasm kindled by Schiller's poetry; his songs were on their lips, and his spirit fought with them."

During the years 1805–11 that struggle brought nothing but disaster to the opponents of Napoleon. The organized might of the French Empire seemed likely to overbear the rest of Europe; and if one investigates the causes of this superiority, they appear to be these: France was the only great nation completely permeated with the new national spirit, and also thoroughly organized for war. The British and Spanish peoples were patriotic, but were ill-organized, while in Napoleon France found the most ruthlessly efficient organizer of all time. The other European States were in a chaotic condition. Austria was a house of cards; Prussia was little better; Russia was honeycombed by corruption. In fact, after the death of Pitt and the dismissal of Stein, Napoleon was confronted by mere mediocrities both in the Cabinet and in the field. Or, to sum up, the new national spirit, born in and after 1804, was a mere infant of days by comparison with the splendid adolescence of France. The experiences of those terrible years prove that the justice of a cause is of little avail unless that cause adapts itself to the needs of the time. If the work of adaptation be slowly and inefficiently carried out, the peoples that are at fault will suffer for their sins of omission. One of the sternest lessons of history is that inefficient and slipshod work, even if it be in the best of causes, must bring disaster. Peoples are punished for slackness and inertia as much as they are for positive crimes. So it was with England, Spain, and Prussia in the years 1804-12. Until they found out Wellington, Scharnhorst, Gneisenau, and Blücher, all the lofty aspirations and enthusiasms were of little avail.

Out of the darkness of despair that brooded over Prussia after the disaster of Jena, one voice sounded forth in words of inspiration and hope. When she lay under the heel of Napoleon; when Berlin and all Prussian cities were garrisoned by French troops, Fichte's easy cosmopolitanism fell from him. Like all noble natures, his was not convinced by conquest. In those dark days he found that he could not transfer his allegiance from Berlin to Paris, though Paris was incontestably supreme, and Berlin seemed to have gone under for ever. Even before the campaign of Jena he addressed the Prussian army in glowing terms; and when it streamed away eastwards towards the Vistula and Niemen in utter rout, his patriotic feelings deepened, as will those of all true men and women in time of anxiety or disaster. Then it was that he discovered cosmopolitanism to be only a fair-weather creed. After the Peace of Tilsit, when Prussia lost half her lands and all her prestige, Fichte stood forth at Berlin, and, within sound of the drums of the French garrison, delivered his "Addresses to the German Nation." They purported to be a continuation of the lectures given in 1804-5; but they breathe an utterly different spirit. For in the interval the idea of nationality laid hold of the popular imagination; and now, too, when the fabric of the Prussian State had fallen in ruin, Fichte saw the German nation. Previously he had discoursed about States: now his theme was far more definite, more human. In face of the Napoleonic ascendancy, what were Prussia and Austria, Saxony and Bavaria? As those miserable divisions had invited disaster, so, too, a close union might bring salvation. The topic was dangerous, as Fichte was well aware: "I know the risk (so he wrote to Beyme in January, 1808). I know that a bullet may strike me down as well as Palm.[1] But that is not what I fear; and, for the aim which I have in view, I too would gladly die."

His aim was to convince Germans everywhere that their present ruin was due to selfishness. Egotism had divided them up into myriads of petty States and kept them divided; so that, what with political barriers and class divisions, they never caught a glimpse of wide and generous aims. He called his age the age of giant selfishness, which had developed to the utmost on all sides and was about to destroy itself. The description is apt if applied to Germany; for, if the Germany of that time was the result of petty selfishness, Napoleon was also the incarnation of colossal acquisitiveness. In the game of grab, into which European politics had degenerated since the accession of Frederick the Great, all trust and confidence had vanished, and thus the great robber-baron beyond the Rhine was able to prey on the thieving knights and footpads of Germany. As yet there was no sign of effective union; for how can there be a firm union among thieves? Fichte was correct in his diagnosis of the disease which paralyzed Europe in 1804-7. Egotism and greed had made of it mere political rubble, and the cement of public confidence was nowhere to be found. Distrust must give way to trust (said Fichte); the old jealousy between German States must vanish in

[1] Palm, a Nürnberg bookseller, was shot by Napoleon's order for the crime of selling a patriotic pamphlet.

view of the urgency of their universal interests; in place of
the class feeling, which had weakened Prussia, there must
arise a national feeling, based on the perception of kindred
aims and duties. Selfishness (said he) is self-destructive; for,
when it has run its full course, no firm foundation is left.
That vice had ruined Germany. How must she be recon-
structed?

Fichte's answer is not altogether clear. It does not sound
forth with the trumpet tones of conviction by which Mazzini
thrilled Italy in the thirties. The German philosopher had not
the abounding faith and enthusiasm of the Italian prophet.
Further, he was hampered by the endeavor to express everything in abstract terms, while Mazzini spoke straight to the
heart of the people. The cloudiness of Fichte's views also resulted from his being a pioneer of thought in this direction—
witness his definition of a nation (Lecture VI)—"A nation is
the whole community of persons living in social intercourse,
ever propagating itself in a natural manner, and existing
collectively under a certain special law of the development of
the divine out of it."

This nebulous circumlocution in no sense advances our
knowledge of the subject; and it must be confessed that the
Addresses are often both dull and confused. Especially tire-
some are Lectures IV–VII, which demonstrate the Germanic
nature of the Germans with an iteration that seems wholly
needless to-day, however much it was needful then to awaken
their dormant national sentiment. After these digressions
Fichte's narrative straightens and broadens. Very effective
is the reference to the ancient Germans, who refused to face
the possibility of being Romanized and were resolved at all
costs to order their lives in their own way. Coming to the
present he lifts the idea of the nation to an eminence whence
it may radiate hope to the myriads of Germans who had
vegetated in little States, one and all now subject to Napoleon.

The following passage in Lecture VIII must have been a revelation to all who could grasp its meaning:—

"Nation and Fatherland in this sense, as bearer of and securer for immortality in this world, and as that which alone here below can be eternal, far transcend the State in the usual sense of that term. . . . This [the State] aims only at security of rights, internal peace, a livelihood to everyone, and preservation of material existence during Heaven's pleasure by means of toil. All this is only the means, condition, preparation for that which patriotism essentially aims at, the blossoming of the eternal and divine in the world. For that very reason, as being the supreme, final, and independent authority, must govern the State itself, while limiting it in the choice of means for its next object, internal peace. With this object in view, the natural freedom of the individual must be restricted in many ways; and, if one has no other intention and aim than this, it would be well to restrict it within the narrowest limits possible."

Idealism here tails off into realism. Fichte's celestial arc ends in a Prussian drill-yard. In later passages he insists on the need of conscription and the drastic restriction of individual liberty. Of course, there were powerful motives why he should urge the claims of Fatherland. It had been ruined by individual selfishness, both of princes and classes. Now, says Fichte, all Germans must think first of the nation and of the duties which they owe to it. No longer must they shift their responsibilities on to someone else. Every man must realize his duty and perform it manfully. For this purpose he will nerve himself by catching a glimpse of what the future may bring to the German nation. He will resolve that the Fatherland shall be absolutely independent of alien rule. Just as the eye can be trained to feel disgust at dirt and disorder, so, too, the political vision of Germans can be quickened until they will reject all thought of subjection to the foreigner. In order to fire them with the heroism neces-

sary for driving out the French, Fichte faces the problem of
the motive power dormant in the will of man. How shall
the ordinary citizen be nerved to the self-abandonment that
can accomplish wonders of bravery? That is the problem.
Evidently, no ordinary motive will suffice. Or, to quote his
words: "Not the spirit of quiet civic obedience to the constitution and the laws. No; but the burning flame of the
higher patriotism which conceives the nation as the embodiment of the eternal, to which the high-minded man joyfully
devotes himself; while the base-minded man, who only exists
for the other, must be compelled to devote himself."

Developing this thought, Fichte seeks to fortify the heroism, even of the high-minded man, by the following inspiring
thought. Such an one will prize his nation above all else;
for it is only the nation which can assure the continuity of his
work. He will value his life, not for the sake of mere existence,
but for the amount of work which he can accomplish; and,
as the nation is the guardian of that work and its guarantor
for the future, he will value its safety far above his own. For
the nation, then, he will gladly lay down his life, so that,
as far as in him lies, he may assure the survival of the larger
life which alone lends significance to his own.[1] The thought
is like that which Kipling, by a flash of genius, has enshrined
in one glorious line:—

"Who dies if England lives?"

It is obvious that Fichte's doctrine as to the absolute
sovereignty of the nation over the lives of all its members
was and is liable to great abuse. Fichte's glowing words
must not blind us to the risk of entrusting the nation for ever
with unlimited powers of life and death.[2] Noble though his

[1] Fichte, Lecture VIII.
[2] See Lord Acton's remarks [*Essays on Liberty*, p. 228] on the Machiavellian traits in Fichte's teaching.

theory may be when the question is of expelling the foreigner,
it becomes pestilential when that task is achieved, and the
nation of death-defying heroes look forth upon less redoubt-
able neighbors. This, as we have seen, was the temptation
that lured Revolutionary France into wars of conquest. A
similar temptation has lured the Germany of William I
into the mad ways of William II.

In the time of Fichte the only question was that of regain-
ing the independence of Germany. But how was it to be
regained? Not by force; that was impossible when the French
held all the fortresses. By moral means, then,—says Fichte
(Lectures IX–XI)—by education; for that is the only domain
in which Napoleon leaves the Germans free. The philosopher
points out that in many respects German education has been
utterly defective. It has been narrow and uninspiring; it
has left its pupils cold and selfish; so that, despite all the
teaching, they have not followed its higher precepts and
warnings, but have gone on following the impulses of their
own natural selfishness. Hitherto education has neither
instructed nor inspired. But its true function is to inspire.
The true educator will not be satisfied with instructing. He
will seek to uplift the moral nature of his students. He will
set forth so glowing a picture of the ideal life that, before it,
cold selfishness will melt away. The moral order of the uni-
verse will appear in so radiant a vision that the petty egotism
of the individual will vanish. And not only the wealthy
and middle classes are to be thus inspired. All classes will
be influenced by the wider and nobler education of the future.
"We desire to inspire Germans by a feeling of unity which
may throb through all their limbs." At this point, as he
catches a vision of what a better training may effect, he doffs
his academic stiffness and exclaims in the inspired words of
Ezekiel: "Come from the four winds, O breath, and breathe
upon these slain, that they may live. So I prophesied, as He

commanded me; and the breath came into them, and they lived, and stood up upon their feet, an exceeding great army."

As to the educational methods to be adopted, Fichte strongly recommended those of the Swiss reformer, Pestalozzi. They were adopted, and, after the infusion of German method, they were found to be of great service. Elementary education, therefore, received an impetus of great value in Prussia; and this development, together with the reforms of Stein, Scharnhorst, and Hardenberg, laid the basis for the healthier polity of the future. In the academic sphere equal progress was made by the establishment of the thoroughly national Universities of Berlin and Breslau (1809–11). An enlightened patriotism watched over them from the start. The King gave a royal palace so that Berlin might have suitable University buildings; and from the nearly bankrupt Treasury 150,000 dollars a year were awarded for the maintenance of the new institution. Hitherto, for the most part, German Universities had existed in small towns remote from political life; and in them there was evolved the type of professor depicted by Carlyle in the person of Diogenes Teufelsdröckh, Professor of Things in General in the University of Weissnichtwo. Readers of *Sartor Resartus* will remember that Teufelsdröckh in the early part of his career was mainly occupied with the cognate employments,—"to think and smoke tobacco." These led him only to the Everlasting No. But in lucid intervals he gradually fought his way towards the Everlasting Yes—"The chief end of life is not thought but action. . . . Up! Up! Whatsoever thy hand findeth to do, do it with thy might."

This surprising change mirrors that which came over the life of Germany in the decade 1804 to 1813. The time of divisions, of sloth, of pleasurable self-seeking passed away; and in its place there came a time marked by terrible suffering and poverty, but irradiated by the noblest deeds of self-sacrifice and heroism. For the most inspired poet and philosopher had spoken to that people in words that burned. Schiller showed what the heroism of unlettered mountaineers could effect in a great and inspiring cause. Fichte, too, after emerging from dreamland, came out into the world of reality and helped to lead his countrymen thither. Emerging from their holes and corners, they discovered their essential oneness; and, as happened to Frenchmen twenty years earlier, the uplift from a narrow provincialism to a sense of nationality endowed them with a buoyancy and vigor never known before. Arndt, Körner, and others composed national songs that stirred the blood; and from the Universities there came professors and students, resolved to win the freedom and independence which Fichte's glowing words had made an essential of life. He, too, formerly so unpractical, sealed the new doctrine with his life-blood; for he died of a fever caught while his wife and he tended the wounded in hospital—an episode as significant as any in the drama of the War of Liberation.

LECTURE IV

THE SPANISH NATIONAL RISING

"C'est de l'Espagne que l'Europe apprit que Napoléon pouvait être vaincu, et comme il pouvait l'être."—TALLEYRAND, *Mémoires*, I, 389.

THE rising of the German people against Napoleon in 1813 is for ever memorable, not only for a heroism finally crowned with well-merited triumph, but also for the work of intellectual and moral preparation, which endowed their national movement with solid backing and permanent results. On turning our thoughts towards the Spanish Peninsula we are conscious of an entire change of conditions, both external and internal. The Spaniards are sometimes reproached with having drawn from that same time of testing, the years 1808–13, none of the beneficent influences that renewed and enriched the life of the German nation. To explain the causes of this divergence is one of my aims in this lecture.

Firstly, Germany held an honored place in the intellectual movement of the eighteenth century. Her leading men, even some of her rulers, were in full sympathy with "Illuminism," which promised peacefully to banish ignorance and to make of mankind one happy family. They welcomed the French Revolution; and only after the perversion of its aims did Teuton and Gaul come into serious conflict. Even when racial animosities were embittered by the Napoleonic occupation, the leaders of thought in Germany continued their efforts, albeit with aims that were distinctly national, not international as of yore. Consequently, eighteenth-century culture did much to invigorate the new life of Central Europe.

Far different was the condition of Spain. She had stood apart from the intellectual movement, which found exponents among a mere handful of her sons. Consequently there were no influential groups of savants, no inspiring traditions, on which the Spanish revival could be based; and, as we shall see, the strange shifts to which their patriots were reduced prevented any well-considered plan of action.

Of all these difficulties the fundamental cause was the aloofness of Spain from Europe. Her aloofness explains not only her intellectual separation, but also her exclusive nationalism. The divergence of her interests from those of her neighbors is due to her insularity. Though seas connect, mountains divide; and the Pyrenees form the most rigid barrier in Europe. No land-power has much influenced the life of Spain, because no land-power has ever been able to control it for long. In the Dark Ages conquerors from the North, Vandals and Visigoths, swept over and even tried to hold the Peninsula. But the effort of the latter people to rule it from Toulouse broke down, just as a similar attempt of Charlemagne broke down. The rugged and impervious barrier of the Pyrenees accounts for the failure. Spain either defied her would-be conquerors from the North, or else she absorbed them.

On the other hand, her Mediterranean coasts almost invite the invader; and she was in succession all but subdued by Carthaginians, Romans, and Moors. But there again, as Livy remarked, the extremes of climate, the barren plateau in the interior, and the wonderful tenacity of the Spaniards in defending their towns rendered complete conquest almost impossible. The Moors, even at the height of their power, never crushed the defenders of the northern fastnesses, who little by little pushed back the invaders, and in the process fashioned the national character to its extremes of valor, bigotry, and pride. Later on, the French monarchs were to experience the toughness of the Spanish nature, and Henri IV summed up their enterprises in the phrase: "In Spain small armies will be beaten, large armies will starve." The memories of conquest of the New World and of invincibility in their own peninsula stiffened the neck of the Spaniards even in the days of their decline. Robert Southey, during his travels in Spain in 1794-5, relates that a Spanish manufacturer who had sought to introduce wheelbarrows into his works could not persuade his men to use them. All kinds of vehicles were meant for beasts of burden, not for Spaniards! The experience of the Italian poet, Alfieri, was the same. He declared the Spaniards to be the only people of Europe "possessed of sufficient energy to struggle against foreign usurpation."

Such was the people whom Napoleon sought to harness to his conqueror's car. In the encyclopædic studies of his youth there is a serious gap. Nowhere does he seem to have studied national character. It was one of the defects of eighteenth-century thought to ignore differences of race. Man was considered as man; and, though Rousseau echoed some of the cautions which Montesquieu had given forth as to those differences, the French Revolutionists paid little heed; and Napoleon certainly erred in assuming that men would in general respond to the same appeals. In his official correspondence is included one letter (dated March 28, 1808) which cautions Murat against ignoring the national energy of the Spaniards; but that letter is a later invention. In the genuine letters there appear no signs even of ordinary caution, as to the risk of provoking the Spaniards. So far as we can judge, Napoleon shared the belief, common in France since the days of Choiseul, that they were a decadent people, negligible as a political force.

This extreme confidence was, perhaps, natural after his conquest of Austria, Prussia, and Russia in the campaigns of 1805–7. England had blundered badly on land; and the Emperor hoped, by means of the new Russian alliance, and thanks to the enforced assistance of the Spanish navy, to reverse the victory of Trafalgar and overthrow even her naval power. Spain, then, he regarded as a tool in the world-wide strife. Early in March, 1808, when Barcelona was scarcely held down by the troops of General Duhesme, the Emperor wrote to Murat: "There is no discontent whatever at Barcelona. General Duhesme is a gossip. . . . On the whole, the people are well disposed, and when we have the citadel, we have everything." Napoleon was then at Paris. He had never been in Spain; yet he claimed to know about the Spaniards better than the French generals then in that country. On April 26, while at Bayonne, he wrote to Murat, at Madrid: "It is time for you to show fitting energy. I expect you will not spare the Madrid mob, if it stirs, and that you will have it disarmed immediately." On April 29 he wrote to the Tsar Alexander I: "These family quarrels [those of Charles IV of Spain with the Heir Apparent, Ferdinand] cause me some trouble; but I will soon be free to arrange the great affair with Your Majesty." [The "great affair" was the partition of Turkey, in which the Spanish fleet was to be serviceable.] After Murat's troops had shot down hundreds of the men of Madrid in the patriotic rising of May 2, the Emperor complimented him on his energy, and announced to him the signature of a treaty with the senile Charles IV at Bayonne, whereby the latter resigned to him (Napoleon) all rights to the throne of Spain. The Estates of Spain would assemble at Bayonne to take suitable measures! All the genuine letters of the time show no sign of apprehension of a national rising in Spain. They are those of a general who believes that he has that people by the throat. Because

French troops occupy Madrid, Barcelona, all the chief northern fortresses, and those of Portugal; because also very many of the Spanish troops are absent either in Portugal or in Holstein, he deems the Spanish problem at an end. For him Spain is the royal family, the Court, the grandees who form the Estates. If he can bully the rightful successor, Ferdinand, into a renunciation of his rights; if he can intern in France both Charles IV and Ferdinand; if he can cajole the Spanish grandees into a recognition of his own claims—then he is master of Spain.

He left out of count one all-important factor—the nation. So soon as the astounding news from Bayonne became known, every town, every province of Spain rejected his sovereignty with scorn and loathing. In vain did Charles and Ferdinand advise submission to the usurper; [1] in vain did the Junta, composed of the leading men of Madrid, inculcate the duty of obeying the new ruler; in vain did the Holy Inquisition preach the same degrading course; in vain did responsible persons and thinkers point out the madness of opposing the master of the Continent. The people rejected the counsels of authority, religion, experience, and reform. With an impulse which was both furious and sustained, both local and universal, they rushed at the French forces and reduced them suddenly to the defensive. District by district, province by province, they rose separately, yet with astounding unanimity. The rising did not begin in Madrid; for the turbulent in that city had been cowed by the cannon and cavalry of Murat. How the same thought or instinct laid hold of the whole of Spain within a few days is a mystery. The episode reminds us of the incalculable forces which now and again have aroused the tribes of Arabia or of the Soudan to united action. Indeed, the Spanish Rising is a recurrence to the ways of primitive man, or at least of the mediæval

[1] *Ann. Register* [1808], p. 214.

levies when the faithful mustered to fight the Moors. Then, as in 1808, the impulse was general, yet the action was provincial. Above all, it was action by the populace. In many places those who had advised submission to the French were butchered without mercy, and patriotic Juntas were chosen by acclamation to arrange for the defence of each province.

Especially noteworthy was the action of that of Asturias. That little province of the North-West was the first to organize a Junta which took decisive action. With splendid audacity that single Junta declared war against Napoleon; and those who notice the connection of the instinct of nationality with the historic sense will remember that in the long warfare against the Moors, Asturias had been the last hope of Spanish freedom. Now it was to be the first hope of the coming national independence. That Junta took another important step. It despatched two deputies to London to beg help from the British people. Legally, Spain was at war with us, as she had been since 1804. But Asturias recked little of legality at such a time. Neither did our great statesman, Canning. The warm welcome accorded by our people to the Asturian deputies revealed to him as by a flash the change that had just come over the spirit of the age. Hitherto (as Sheridan finely said) "Bonaparte had run a victorious race because he had contended against princes without dignity, ministers without wisdom, and countries where the people were indifferent as to his success." Clearly a new age had dawned when a provincial Council dared to throw down the gauntlet to the great Emperor.

I have failed to find in the British archives an account either of Canning's interview with the two delegates or of the Cabinet meeting where the decision was formed to help the Spanish people. It must have been formed very quickly; for on June 15 Canning spoke as follows in the

House of Commons: "We shall proceed upon the principle that any nation of Europe that starts up to oppose a Power, . . . the common enemy of all nations, whatever be the existing political relations of that nation, it becomes instantly our essential Ally." In pursuance of this definitely national policy, Great Britain on July 4 ordered the cessation of hostilities with Spain; and there ensued an informal but binding alliance with the Spanish people. There was an inner fitness in this compact; for it bound together the only States which then were conterminous with nations. Napoleonic France had far outleaped her natural bounds. The British and Spanish peoples now undertook to restrain her within just limits; and the potency of the national impulse is seen in the rally of every people in Europe to their side in the years 1812–14.

The Anglo-Spanish Alliance is, therefore, a turning point in the long struggle against Napoleon. Up to the year 1807 he had embodied the genius and strength of Revolutionary France; and her strength (at once democratic and national) far exceeded that of the torpid and artificial States around her. But now, from motives of ambition, he went out of his way to interfere with a people that only asked to be left alone; and his conduct aroused in it a hatred that nothing could quench. Consequently, the national impulse, which had helped France to overthrow the moribund States of Italy and Germany, now began to operate against her; and even the military genius of Napoleon could not make up for the downward drag which this fatal incubus entailed. No campaigns were so much detested by the French soldiery as those in Spain; and that, not so much because they had to face Wellington and the Spanish climate, as on account of the savage hatred which they encountered from the Spaniards themselves. The outcome of that hatred will appear in the following passages, taken from the first

Proclamation of the Supreme Junta. After recounting some successes of the Spaniards and advising a war of partisans, the appeal thus refers to the memory of the glorious past.

"France has never domineered over us, nor set her foot in our territory. We have many times mastered her, not by deceit, but by force of arms; we have made her Kings prisoners, and we have made that nation tremble; we are the same Spaniards; and France and Europe and the world shall see that we are not less gallant than the most glorious of our ancestors."

The proclamation then states that when their lawful King, Ferdinand, is restored

"the Cortes will be assembled, abuses reformed, and such laws be enacted as the circumstances of the time and experience may dictate for the public good and happiness—things which we Spaniards know how to do, which we have done as well as other nations, without any necessity that the vile French should come to instruct us; and, according to their custom, under the mask of friendship and wishes for our happiness, should contrive to plunder us, to violate our women, to assassinate us, to deprive us of our liberty, our laws, and our King, to scoff at and destroy our holy religion. . . ." [1]

That is an official document. As for the pamphlets of the time, let this suffice. It is a retort to Napoleon's offer of reforms, beginning with the usual formula: "Napoleon, Emperor of the French, King of Italy, Protector of the Confederation of the Rhine," etc. The counterblast begins:—

"Yes! Napoleon, that is Napo-dragon, Apollyon, Ruler of the Abyss, King of the monsters of Hell, heretics, and heretic princes,— Abominable Beast, Protector, Head and Soul of the Confederation

[1] *Ibid.*, pp. 218, 219.

of the Rhine, that is of the seven heads and ten horns of the beast, which bear blasphemies against God and the Saints. . . ."

Thus religion was now invoked against the French. For this the Emperor had himself to thank. As if his Spanish business were not enough, he in that same springtime despoiled the Pope of four provinces. In consequence, Pius VII anathematized his despoiler, and urged the Spaniards to arise like David and slay Goliath. The Spanish Rising therefore partook of the nature of a crusade. Their armies were placed under the protection of saints, and in some cases relics of saints went with them to battle, thereby inflaming the Spanish nature to its utmost.

All these aids were needed; for in a military sense Spain was almost defenceless. Her regular troops were, in the main, absent; her capital and chief fortresses were held by the French; there was no one centre of union for the various provinces, which soon fell to quarrelling about the allocation of the money and stores sent from England. Indeed, Spain was in a worse plight than France was before the Battle of Valmy; but the same potent impulse nerved the defenders; and, fortunately for the Spanish patriots, Napoleon's eagerness to seize the fleet at Cadiz (including the French ships that escaped from Trafalgar) led him prematurely to press on a large French force towards that port. It was surrounded, overborne, and compelled to surrender at Baylen (July, 1808). What Valmy had been to France, Baylen was to Spain, a proof that she could overcome troops hitherto deemed invincible.

In one respect the Spanish victory at Baylen was a misfortune. It filled the Spaniards with intolerable conceit. When Joseph Bonaparte and the French troops fell back behind the line of the Ebro, the perfervid imagination of the South saw in fancy the standards of Spain soaring over the Pyrenees and entering the plains of Guienne. Napier relates that the Spanish officers remarked to those of Sir John Moore's army: " We are much obliged to our friends, the English; we thank them for their good will; we shall escort them through France to Calais; . . . they shall not have the trouble of fighting the French; and we shall be pleased to have them as spectators of our victories."[1] This lofty spirit went before a terrible fall. In the autumn and winter of 1808 Napoleon burst in on these cackling fowl and scattered them to the winds. Yet, even so, Spain was not conquered. After every defeat she rose, still defiant. The defence of her walled towns, especially Saragossa, was sublime; and that defence was conducted by the people themselves, no less than by the military. Fifty French cannon during forty days played upon its walls and massive monasteries before the eagles of Napoleon floated over the ruins of the capital of Aragon.

It was both the weakness and the strength of the Spaniards that their national sense was largely provincial. It was their weakness because the provinces rarely worked well together. The different Juntas were absurdly jealous as well as greedy. Besides, owing to the occupation of Madrid by the enemy, there was no possibility of direction from a central point. Further, the haughty and suspicious nature of the Spaniards rendered cordial co-operation with Wellington extremely difficult. Hence the Duke, after Talavera, left them alone and operated from Portugal as a base. Not until Napoleon's Grand Army perished in Russia was there a chance of beating the French in Spain. But then, in 1813, after numerous defeats had rendered the natives more reasonable, all the forces of the Peninsula pulled well together. The results were phenomenal, and French domination vanished in the brief campaign of Vittoria.

[1] *Napier*, I, 84.

Nevertheless, the provincial sentiment also strengthened the Spanish cause; for when one province was lost, the others resisted none the less stoutly; and the task of the French in holding down a population that scorned surrender increased with every success. As Marshal Jourdan wrote: "The more soundly the Spanish armies were beaten, the more eagerly did that people rush to arms; the more the French gained ground, the more dangerous did their position become." The broken and inhospitable nature of the country singularly favored the partisan warfare of the defenders, so that, provided Wellington held a large French force to the West, and all the other provinces persevered, the ultimate failure of the French was inevitable. Even the genius of Napoleon could not break down the alliance of the Spanish national spirit with the great Sea Power. Moreover, the display of this tenacious vitality in a land hitherto deemed moribund created a profound impression amidst every nation of the world.

Spain derived little permanent benefit from all this expenditure of energy; and the reason for this disappointing finale seems to be that the Spanish movement differed *in toto* from that of France nineteen years before. In its essence the French Revolution was a revolt of the brain of France against a cramping system which she had long outgrown. In 1808 it was not the brain, but the heart of Spain which led to action; and the action was directed solely against foreign invaders or usurpers. The Spanish Rising offers an example of nationalism in its most passionate form. It is, on a large scale, the action of a family, which seeks to expel intruders who have violated its hospitality. In such a case we do not expect the family immediately to set about the reform of its internal economy. Long before the events of 1789 France (if we may pursue our simile) had been outgrowing its ancestral abode, and the call for

reconstruction and refitting was imperative. The case of
Spain was utterly different. Therefore, to reproach the
Spaniards for not making so good a use as the French of
the opportunity offered by an outburst of national zeal
is manifestly unfair.

Nevertheless, the Spaniards did attempt to make some
changes, though in a somewhat hurried and one-sided way.
The defects of their procedure resulted from two dominant
facts. They had to legislate at Cadiz; and at that city,
within sound of the roar of Marshal Soult's guns, deputies
of the unconquered provinces could assemble freely; but
refugees from the large portions of territory held by the
French were accepted as representatives of those unfortunate towns and districts. Naturally, such a haphazard
assemblage did not evince qualities of prudence and good
sense, but rather of passion and prejudice. Naturally, too,
it was violently anti-French; and yet this very body, almost
of necessity, borrowed from France the groundwork for
the new constitution. As the English constitution was too
vague to appeal to Continental reformers, those of Cadiz
fell back upon the example set by the French Constituent
Assembly in 1791. They restricted the functions of their
future King within narrow limits; and, copying the phrase-
ology of the Rights of Man, they declared that "sovereignty
resided essentially in the nation." In this view of things,
Ferdinand VII, when restored, would be merely the first
magistrate of the land. Further, the men of Cadiz swept
away Feudalism root and branch, dissolved the monastic Orders, and abolished the Inquisition. This servile imitation of
the French legislators of 1789-91 at once produced sharp
friction; and Ferdinand, after his restoration in 1814, found
it easy to abrogate this imported constitution. Thus the
misuse of the national idea by a few extremists at Cadiz,
was destined to work infinite harm both to Spain herself

and to the cause of democracy and nationality so unwisely championed. But it is only fair to remember that that cause had not a fair chance amidst the storms and excitements of so wholly exceptional an epoch.

Despite its obvious faults, the Spanish constitution of 1812 aroused much enthusiasm among neighboring peoples. During the period of reaction and despair which followed the downfall of Napoleon, the "Carbonari" of France and Italy and the "Liberales" of Spain continued to strive for the strange compromise of 1812; and it took tangible form during a few months in Spain, Portugal, and Italy at the time of the democratic risings of 1820–2. Those risings failed; for the Austrian and other autocratic rulers (Louis XVIII among them) intervened to crush them; but the memories of popular liberty in Spain during the years 1812–3 lived on; and, amidst the gloom of the time of reaction, the Spanish constitution of those years aroused fond recollections and hopes for the future. Especially was this so in Naples and Sicily, where the Spanish movement of the Napoleonic time helped on that which is associated with the names of Mazzini and Garibaldi.

If the Spanish movement of 1808–13 bears only a superficial resemblance to that of revolutionary France, still more did it diverge from that of Germany. We have already noticed one cause of that divergence, but others will now occur to us. Napoleon imposed his supremacy on the Germans piecemeal and with some measure of caution. On the neck of the proudest people of Europe he forced his yoke with sudden and almost contemptuous insolence. Consequently, while the uprising of the Germans was not unlike the mounting of a tide over sandbanks, that of the Spaniards resembled an explosion. The difference was also due to diversities of national character and environment. The Spaniard was proud and resentful; the German of the eighteenth century was torpid and diffident. During four centuries the Spaniards had formed a nation. The average Teuton could neither remember nor imagine a time when all his people were united. The political helplessness of Germany led her sons to a humorous depreciation—witness these lines of Goethe's *Faust*, when the boon companions in Auerbach's cellar troll the catch:—

> "The Holy Roman Empire now
> How holds it together?"

And again:—

> "Thank God, every morn,
> To rule the Roman Empire, that you were not born.
> I bless my stars at least that mine is not
> Either a Kaiser's or a Chancellor's lot."

No Spaniard would ever have sung those lines about the compact and glorious kingdom which had conquered, and still ruled over, the greater part of the New World. Nature, which had made the Spaniards a nation, seemed, until the year 1812, to doom the Germans to division and helplessness. During the winter of 1807–8 Prussia's boldest son, Fichte, did not counsel revolt, only a system of national education with a view to some eventual revolt. The German movement therefore was no flash of passion, but rather the growth of an intellectual and moral conviction that Germany must some day form a nation. In the spread of that belief, which became contagious when Napoleon's Grand Army reeled back frostbitten from Russia, lie the unique interest and the exceptional fruitfulness of the German movement. Heralded by a poet and a philosopher, it uplifted the people and bore them to a higher plane of existence. The national policy of the years 1808–13 began by improving and inspiring the individual; it ended by making an intelligent and valiant nation.

The blaze of wrath which flashed forth in Spain in 1808 could not mature her national life. That life was scorched, not ripened. No literary work of any note was forthcoming; and, apart from the abolition of Feudalism, no lasting reforms resulted from the sudden and premature efforts of that time. For lack of preparation or wise guidance the national movement at Cadiz and Madrid went astray, and ended in political reaction. The case of Spain, therefore, proves that an appeal to the past, and to a pride rooted in that past, may incite a people to great exertions; but, whatever their military results, they will have no effect on its development, and may drag it backwards. In short, nationality in its crudest form is merely an appeal to the emotions or passions and may arrest the progress of a people that indulges them. Under wise and strict control, as in the Germany of those years, it may further the cause of progress. In the case of revolutionary France, and still more of Spain, nationality was a narrowing influence, begetting intolerance towards neighbors and promoting the interests of despotism at home.

These, I think, are the conclusions to be drawn from a survey of the Spanish movement in its wider issues. But now let us consider it, finally, in its bearing on the Napoleonic Wars. In that respect its importance can scarcely be overrated. The spectacle of a nation challenging to mortal conflict a powerful enemy that occupied her chief cities and had filched away her King stirred the blood of all nations, as does the sight of gallant little Serbia holding up against two military Empires on the North and her perfidious neighbor on the East.[1] Moreover, the success of the Spanish efforts in the summer of 1808 at Baylen and Saragossa roused an excitement unequalled in that generation. The spell of invincibility that had long protected the French and bewildered their foes was broken, and forlorn peoples caught a gleam of hope.

[1] These words were spoken early in November, 1915.

Germany, then writhing under the heel of Napoleon, ceased to despair. In October, 1808, the writer, Varnhagen von Ense, visiting his *confrère*, Jean Paul Richter, heard him say that he never doubted that the Germans would one day rise against the French as the Spaniards had done. "The Spaniards were the refrain to everything, and we always returned to them." The statesman, Stein, actually prepared for a popular rising in Prussia like that of Spain, and when found out was driven from office and from Prussia by the order of Napoleon. Austria, whose subjects had fought against the French hopelessly and nervelessly, early in 1809 made a really national effort. In April the Archduke Charles issued this stirring appeal: "The liberty of Europe has taken refuge under your banners. Your victories will loose its fetters, and your brothers in Germany, yet in the ranks of the enemy, long for their deliverance."

These hopes and aspirations were directly the outcome of the Spanish Rising. It is true that neither Spain nor Austria succeeded in those years. The Spaniards displayed no skill in organization and proved to be very exasperating allies. The Austrian Government and its generals behaved with their usual want of energy and enterprise. In both lands the spirit of the people far excelled the conduct of Governments and generals. But such a symptom bodes ill for the enemy. For ultimately the energy and determination of the people will find leaders to give full effect to its resolves; and that happened in 1813–5. By that time the new national feelings of Spain and Germany were incarnated in formidable armies led by the ablest of their generals.

During the four intervening years, generally marked by defeat, the fortitude of all patriots was tried to the uttermost. It may be well to recall the feelings of those dark days when the Napoleonic supremacy seemed irresistible.

In May, 1809, the *Quarterly Review* thus described the situation:—

"A more tremendous system never appeared for the desolation and subjection of the world. Every country was to be compelled in succession to furnish men for the plunder and conquest of others. If any one nation presumed to be dissatisfied, the population of another was to be driven to arms to oppress it. . . . Napoleon's vast designs have been executed with the most lavish profusion of human blood. He cares neither for distance, famine, nor disease. . . . It is indifferent to him how many thousands of his troops drop from mere fatigue and want. It is sufficient that enough reach the point of action to accomplish his purposes. If he disperses the enemy, he gains a new extent of population to drive into his ranks, and to make the instruments, however unwilling, of new depredations. Being consumed so fast, there is no time for mutiny and little demand for pay. For a certain time, therefore, this terrible engine of war acts in his favor with dreadful energy, though it is one which may ultimately recoil upon himself."

Five weary years were to elapse before the spirit of nationality was completely embattled. Then it overthrew the great Emperor. In that time of awakening the people of Spain hold a foremost place; for they dared to beard the conqueror in his prime. Before they knew that England would help them they challenged the master of the Continent, Thus, once again, Europe showed the diversity of racial impulses that go to make up its life. The balance of that life has been in succession restored by races as far removed, as widely dissimilar, as the Franks, Dutch, English, Swedes, Poles, Spaniards, and Russians. The motives prompting these efforts were very different. Byron thus outlined the Spanish Rising: "Pride points the way to Liberty." That is true. The proud and passionate resentment of the Spaniards led the more phlegmatic peoples of the North into the crusade that finally overthrew the might of Napoleon.   So long as the British and Spaniards held firmly together, he could not conquer Europe; for it is of the very nature of World-Policy that, sooner or later, it provokes world-wide resistance.   All honor to the two nations that first dared to offer an unbending resistance.

LECTURE V

MAZZINI AND YOUNG ITALY

"Every people has its special mission, which will co-operate towards the fulfilment of the general mission of Humanity. That mission constitutes its nationality. Nationality is sacred."— *Mazzini*, 1834.

OUR previous studies have, I think, pointed to the conclusion, that no popular movement has led to results of lasting importance, unless it proceeded from some formative thought. If it be true, as Carlyle says, that the end of man is action, not thought, it is equally true that the beginning of all action is a thought; and the usefulness of the action corresponds to the correctness of the thought. Only where the thinkers have led the masses, and led them aright, has the resulting movement been well sustained and healthful in its effects. Where, as in the case of the Spanish Rising of 1808, the impulse has been that of outraged pride and dignity, unconnected with the deeper convictions of the mind, little has come of it. An explosion of terrific force took place, but thereafter everything tended to settle down in nearly the same condition as before. That is nationality in its elemental form, an almost blind impulse, which cannot lead to continued progress, and may even retard progress.

But now we turn to a land where the popular impulse found wise and inspiring leaders. A cynic once called the Italian national movement "the poetry of politics." The taunt veiled a truth; for that movement initiated not only the poetry but the philosophy of modern politics.

Nearly all movements start as a protest against a wrong; and the Italian movement is no exception to the rule. The people of the Peninsula struggled against the barriers imposed on them by the Treaties of Vienna of 1814–5, which divided and enslaved them. A consciousness of their oneness had grown among them during the Napoleonic régime, when unity of administration and comradeship in arms evoked a sense of manliness and citizenship. As Mrs. Browning phrased it:—

> "Children use the fist, until they are of age
> To use the brain, . . .
> And so we needed Cæsars to assist
> Man's justice, and Napoleons to explain
> God's counsel."

In 1815 came the cruel awakening. On a neck straightening with national pride there now fell the yoke of two kings, a Pope, four dukes, and, worst of all, the military despotism of Austria in the North and North-East. It was in vain that Italians resisted. Austria, encamped in her Quadrilateral, and strengthened by her Italian satraps, defied all the puny efforts of the subject race. In vain did the Carbonari strike down a general here, a police officer there, they could not drive out the white coats of Austria. All the tyrants made common cause; and, if one of them were in danger, the Hapsburgs sent down their legions to restore "order." As the mandatory of the Holy Alliance, Austria repressed not only every movement of the people but every proposal of an Italian ruler to admit them to the least share in the Government. She would neither reform herself nor let any Italian State reform itself, for fear that her rule might seem the more odious by the contrast.[1] In fact, the House of Hapsburg now became the chief barrier to

[1] Farini, *The Roman State*, I, ch. I.

national aspirations in Europe; and its Chancellor, Metternich, occupied the position formerly occupied by Napoleon as the deadliest enemy of nationality. The Hapsburgs held down their Magyar and Slavonic subjects; they barred the way to an effective union of the German States; above all, they played the watch-dog to the sheepfolds in which the Italians were penned up. Austria strove to stifle thought in her dominions, as appeared in the injunction of the Emperor Francis to the professors of the University of Pavia: "Your duty is less to make learned men than faithful subjects." Consequently, every Italian patriot longed to drive the Austrians beyond the Alps. On this topic there was practical unanimity. On all else there were grave differences.

Putting aside smaller groups, we may single out from the patriots three parties: (1) Those who desired the supremacy of the Pope; (2) those who championed the cause of the House of Savoy; (3) Republicans who desired the end both of monarchy and of the Temporal Power of the Popes, in order to frame an Italian Republic.

The first party pointed to the services which the Popes had often rendered to the Italian cause, e. g. to the Holy League which Julius II formed in 1510 for the expulsion of the foreigners from Italy. Naturally enough, they left out of count the occasions when the Papacy had sided with foreigners against the Italian cause; and the armed support which was consistently claimed from Austria by Gregory XVI during his pontificate (1831–46), alienated the respect of all patriots. Nevertheless, the mystical devotion of a priest, Gioberti, pointed to the Papacy as the rallying point for Italians. This was the theme of his book, *The Moral and Civil Supremacy of the Italians* (1843), a work which made a deep impression and contributed largely towards the election of a reforming Pope, Pius IX, in 1846.

The second party had its headquarters at Turin, and refused to admit a Papal hegemony. Even after the advent of a popular and reforming pontiff, they held to the belief that the House of Savoy alone could bring union or complete unity to the Peninsula. They pointed to the deep-seated abuses of clerical government in the Papal States, where only ten per cent of the people could read; also to the fact that those States, stretching from the Adriatic to the Tyrrhene Sea, cut off the North from the South of Italy, and barred the way to political union. Finally, they claimed that their royal house, traditionally brave and patriotic, was the natural champion of Italy against Austria, and therefore the only hope of freedom and independence. The monarchists of Piedmont did not at first openly aim at national unity; for such an avowal would have exposed the House of Savoy to the charge of mere ambition. Ostensibly, then, their aim was to federalize Italy under the ægis of that dynasty; but the bolder spirits, headed by Cavour, always kept unity before them as the goal. Such a consummation was anathema to Gioberti and the neo-Guelfs. Looking to the Pope as head of a future Italian federation, they perforce rejected the idea of Italian unity. Nationalism, however, was the very breath of life to a third party, the Mazzinians, or Young Italy.

Joseph Mazzini, born at Genoa in 1805, matured his precocious intelligence in the decades following Waterloo, when Italy underwent the torture of division and servitude. Endowed with a highly sensitive nature, he hated the kings and dukes who divided and held down his people. As he wrote in 1831: "There is not one of these princes who has not signed a compact with Austria in the blood of his subjects; not one whose past life is not a violent and insurmountable barrier between him and the future of his people." As for Charles Albert, King of Sardinia, his timidity and vacillation finally brought him into the position of a renegade to the patriotic cause; and the young enthusiast even connived at an attempt at his assassination. A theist by conviction, Mazzini detested the Papacy on religious no less than political grounds. Further, the failure of the "moderates" in 1831, and their cowardly abandonment by Louis Philippe, filled him with contempt for constitutional monarchy and all political compromises. Accordingly, during his time of exile at Marseilles in the autumn of that year, he matured the republican organization known as Young Italy.

The name indicates its character. Despairing of the men of advanced years, who were nearly all "moderates"; despairing, too, of all help from France and England, where dull moderation sat enthroned, Mazzini appealed in burning words to the youth of Italy to raise the red, white, and green flag for the Republic and for national unity. In the first document of the Association he explained what he meant by a nation and also the Italian nation: "By the nation we understand the totality of Italians bound together by a common pact and governed by the same laws." This definition marks a great advance on that of Fichte and all previous thinkers. The only objection to it is the emphasis which it lays on Rousseau's idea of a common pact, which is certainly not essential to the forming of a nation.

Equally significant are the boundaries of the future Italian State. They will be from the River Var, in Nice, to Trieste on the North-East, and will comprise the Trentino; also "the islands proved Italian by the language of the inhabitants." This description would include Corsica and several islands of the Adriatic; but it is worthy of note that Mazzini did not claim for Italy the Dalmatian coast-line, which he knew to be Slavonic, not Italian. Though there is a veneer of Italian culture in some of the towns on the coast, yet the great body of the population is Slavonic, closely akin to the Serbs, or, in the North, to the Croats. It is, therefore, certain that Mazzini, if he were now alive, would heartily approve of Italy attacking Austria in order to recover the Trentino and Trieste; but he would disapprove of those eager patriots who hanker after the Dalmatian coast because it once belonged to Venice. In his eyes the historic argument weighs light as against the instincts of the people concerned. We can imagine his scorn at the argument that Italy must have Dalmatia because she has no good harbor in the Adriatic. He decides the question on the ground of nationality, not on the naval considerations which have so often worked mischief. He claims for Italy only those islands where the inhabitants are Italian. Thus his nationalism is thoroughly fair as between Italians and Slavs. He leaves the Slavonic islands and all the lands East of the Adriatic to the Slavs; and, if the Italians are wise enough to recognize that those islands and all the Dalmatian coast are properly Slavonic, not Italian, Europe will avoid complications that may in the future lead to war.

Mazzini then explained that Italy ought to be a Republic, because there were no truly monarchical elements in the Peninsula, and her best epochs were those of republican rule. Further, an Italian monarchy would be reduced to bargain with and imitate other Courts; whereas Mazzini detested compromise with and imitation of foreigners, as certain to weaken and degrade Italy's mission to mankind. His soaring idealism also rejected both the federal schemes and insisted on unity as the aim of Italian strivings. The Pope in the centre, the two kings at the extremities, the Austrians in the North-East and their four ducal satraps—all must go, because they hindered that absolutely free intercourse of the people which was essential to the full development of the Italian Family. To divide it up under eight different governments would be equivalent to tying the body-politic with so many ligaments fatal to the free circulation of the blood.

Mazzini had boundless faith in human nature and its lofty destinies. In his view the life of the human race was essentially one. True, there were great differences between this and that race. He never held Fichte's early opinion, that all the nations were alike, and followed the same aims. He regarded them as members of the great human family, not rivals engaged in ceaseless competition and strife. He also hoped that, if the members were allowed free play, they would come to see their true interests towards each other and to the family of which they formed a part. But, said he, they could not see this truth if they led a cramped and artificial existence. Therefore, Italy must attain to her free life, not for any selfish purpose; certainly not in order to invade and despoil her neighbors, but rather that she may minister to their welfare. She will gain unity for the purpose of carrying out her mission to other nations.

As to the nature of that mission Mazzini nowhere gave a definite answer. In the programme of Young Italy he pointed out that Europe was undergoing a series of changes destined to transform European Society into large and compact masses. The large States, or federations of States, were absorbing small States; large towns were growing at the expense of small towns or villages: the big factory was superseding the small workshop and cottage industries. What would be the upshot of it all? Would the new agglomerations be peaceful or aggressive, healthy or noxious? That was an urgent question, and it still is. How Italy could help to solve these political and social problems Mazzini does not explain. Later on, he felt his way towards a partial answer. Meanwhile he insisted on Italy gaining an unfettered existence. This he defined as follows: "Without unity of religious belief and unity of social pact; without unity of civil, political, and penal legislation, there is no true nation."

The ideal is lofty. Unity of religious belief is hard to attain and keep in the modern world; and it is strange that one who had broken away from the Roman Catholic Church should postulate it as essential. Again, legal unity is desirable, but scarcely attainable without doing violence to local customs. Mazzini's requirements would also rule out Switzerland from the list of nations. Yet, as we have seen, the Swiss form a nation. His aim, doubtless, was to hold up a lofty ideal which should inspire Piedmontese, Venetians, Tuscans, Romans, and Neapolitans with a passion for self-sacrifice. Nothing short of utter self-sacrifice could nerve them to the colossal task of breaking their eight prison-houses and forming a national home. What a task! To expel Austria, to destroy the Temporal Power of the Papacy, and to dethrone six Italian sovereigns. What wonder that he pitched his aims high! The fault of all his predecessors lay in their proneness to bargain and compromise—tactics which gained some outside help but stifled the enthusiasm of Italia's sons. Mazzini sought to arouse that enthusiasm. It throbs in every sentence of the oath which Young Italy imposed at initiation:—

"In the name of God and of Italy. In the name of all the martyrs of the holy Italian cause who have fallen beneath foreign and domestic tyranny. . . . By the love I bear to the country that gave my mother birth, and will be the home of my children. . . . By the blush that rises to my brow when I stand before the citizens of other lands, to know that I have no rights of citizenship, no country, and no national flag. By the memory of our former greatness, and the sense of our present degradation. By the tears of Italian mothers for their sons dead on the scaffold, in prison, or in exile. By the sufferings of the millions—I swear to dedicate myself wholly and for ever to strive to constitute Italy one free, independent, republican nation."

Such was the enterprise undertaken by a group of penniless Italian exiles at Marseilles in the autumn of 1831. They aimed at arousing Italians, whether in Italy or South America,[1] to a sense of duty to the nation; and out of their slender means they started a journal, *Young Italy*. When expelled from France by Louis Philippe's Government, they sought refuge in Switzerland; and a few of them attempted a raid into Piedmont which completely failed. In fact, most of their undertakings were so ill-timed and imprudent, as to lead to a useless effusion of blood. But nothing could long daunt Mazzini. Whether hunted about Switzerland, or vegetating in distress among Italian organ-grinders in Hatton Garden, he (with the exception of some dark hours of doubt and despair) maintained a firm resolve to persevere in his quest.

This fixed determination was fed from diverse sources. His nature, though intensely nervous and far from strong, was singularly buoyant. It rallied soon, even after trials and reverses that depressed men of sounder physique. His mind, too, possessed that sharp edge, that rigid grip, which fortified him against disappointment. Under soft and almost feminine features there worked a powerful brain, a steel-like will. Moreover, his personality brought him troops of friends. His conversation charmed and delighted all who came near him. Men so diverse in character as Carlyle, George Meredith, and Joseph Cowen of Newcastle, acknowledged the spell of his presence. Meredith, in *Vittoria*, speaks ecstatically of his "large, soft, dark, meditative eyes," which drew in the soul of the observer into the midst of a

[1] In Uruguay, Joseph Garibaldi [born at Nice in 1807] was won back for the Italians by Mazzini's propaganda.

"capacious and vigorous mind"; of his smile which "came softly as a curve in water," which "seemed to flow with and to pass in and out of his thoughts, to be a part of his emotion and his meaning when it shone transiently full. For, as he had an orbed mind, so he had an orbed nature." Mrs. Hamilton King, in that inspired poem, *The Disciples*, tells enthusiastically how

> "the orb of that great human soul
> Did once deflect and draw this orb of mine
> Until it touched and trembled on the line
> By which my orbit crossed the plane of his."

And Swinburne, in *A Song of Italy*, hails him as the first of her liberators. He hymns the Italians as:

> "Thy children, ev'n thy people thou hast made,
> Thine, with thy words arrayed,
> Clothed with thy thoughts, and girt with thy desires,
> Yearn up towards thee like fires."

Not that Mazzini was devoid of faults of character. They were the excess of his qualities, but some of them were serious. His convictions were so intense as to blind him often to the good advice of others. Hence he was often intolerant towards those who differed from him. But these defects belong rather to Mazzini, the man of action, than to Mazzini, the thinker; and we are concerned solely with his political thought, not with his many abortive conspiracies or even with his highest achievement, the administration of the Roman Republic of 1849.

In this sphere of thought he had one great advantage over his German predecessors. They were so obsessed by the idea of the State as to work their way tardily and doubtfully to the idea of the nation. This was natural. In modern

Germany the Prussian State overshadowed everything else; and under it the German nation loomed nebulous. There-fore, the German thinkers on nationality (except during the ill-starred democratic efforts of 1848-9) tended to Prussianize their notions and often became hide-bound bureaucrats. Not so with the Italians. They were not overshadowed by the Sardinian State; and they detested every other State of the Peninsula. Consequently, the political thought of Italy was free from the distracting influence of the State idea. The Italian thinkers, including Balbo, Cavour, Ma-miani, and Gioberti, saw the nation clearly; and for them the State was merely the concrete embodiment of the na-tional idea. In Germany the national idea was Prussianized, to its infinite harm. The Italian idea was never in danger of being Sardinianized; though Mazzini, amidst the disap-pointments of old age, declared that to have been its fate.

During his manhood, Mazzini not only saw clearly, but believed absolutely in, the nation. The story of Italy's past as well as her natural tendencies to unity combined to nurture in him a profound belief in her future. In common with all thinkers who have exercised a lasting influence on their fellows, he was pre-eminently a man of faith; and his creed for Italy aroused a unique fervor, because it formed part of a far wider creed—the Gospel of Humanity. No-where does he describe the creed in set terms. No prophet ever does. But we catch a glimpse of his meaning in these words:—

"When in my earliest years I believed that the *initiative* of the third life of Europe would spring from the heart, the action, the enthusiasm, and the sacrifices of our people, I heard within me the grand voice of Rome sounding once again; its utterances treasured up and accepted with loving reverence by the peoples, and telling of moral unity and fraternity in a faith common to all Human-ity. . . . I saw Rome in the name of God and a republican Italy

substituting a Declaration of Principles for the sterile Declaration
of Rights; . . . and I saw Europe, weary of scepticism, egotism,
and anarchy, accept the new faith with acclamations."

The Genoese republican here speaks almost with the tongue
of the old monarchist of Florence. This neo-Roman creed
is a modern version of the *De Monarchiâ* of Dante. Rome
(not the city of the Popes but the centre of a world-republic)
calls the peoples about her to listen to the voice of faith and
authority, faith in the perfectibility of man, authority inherent in the genius of the eternal City. A dream, you will
say. Well! a glorious dream. It inspired Mazzini to struggle
on through a life full of disaster, until, as he breathed his
last at Pisa in 1872, his ideals lay shattered by collision with
coarse reality. That faith must have been intense which
impelled him forward, and which, working through him,
impelled many thousands of Italians to endure prison, exile,
torture, and execution for the cause. An intense faith like
his evades mere analysis. Cold criticism misses the soul of
it. If we ask—What do you mean by your neo-Romanism?—
we receive an inadequate answer. The disciple may reply—
Rome has twice given laws to the world, once through the
matchless organization of the old Empire, and again through
the decrees of the Church; therefore she is destined a third
time to initiate an era for mankind. "Not proven," the
logician will say. "Contrary to the tendencies of Vatican
policy," the historian will say. Mazzini and his disciples
ignored both objectors. The eye of faith saw Rome rid herself of Vaticanism and with magical power gather Italians
about her in order to revivify the life of all peoples.

The conception was not wholly visionary. Mazzini was
convinced that French democrats at the time of the great
Revolution had gone utterly astray. That is the meaning
of his phrase, "the sterile Declaration of Rights," a reference

to the Declaration of the Rights of Man drawn up by the Constituent Assembly in August–September, 1789. In its place Rome, the true birth-place of law, was to sound forth a Declaration of the Duties of Man.

This is the bed-rock of Mazzinian doctrine. Let us test it. He declares the French Rights of Man to be sterile; and elsewhere he terms that programme false, hurtful, the mother of selfishness and strife. Thus, in *Faith and the Future* (1835):—

"Right [1] is the faith of the individual. Duty is the common collective faith. Right can but organize resistance; it may destroy, it cannot found. Duty builds up, associates, and unites; it is derived from a general law, whereas Right is derived only from human will. There is nothing, therefore, to forbid a struggle against Right. Any individual may rebel against any Right of another individual which is injurious to him; and the sole judge between the adversaries is force; and such, in fact, has frequently been the answer which societies based upon Right have given to their opponents. Societies based upon Duty would not be compelled to have recourse to force. Duty, once admitted as the rule, excludes the possibility of struggle, and by rendering the individual subject to the general aim, it cuts at the very root of those evils which Right is unable to prevent. . . . The doctrine of Rights puts an end to sacrifice and cancels martyrdom from the world."

Such is the moral elevation of this teaching that we are apt at first to overlook its good sense. But students of the French Revolution, who look beneath the surface of events, will realize the truth of Mazzini's criticism. The fact that the reformers of 1789 laid stress only upon the Rights of Man produced at once the wrong kind of impression both on the

---

[1] Mazzini in this passage uses the term "Right" as equivalent to "The theory of individual Rights."

deputies and the people at large. They were led to regard politics as a struggle in which you seize what you can for your class and yourself. In the course of such a struggle the rights of others are disregarded; they resist; and the only method of deciding the issue is in the last resort by tumult or by civil war. To emphasize the rights of the individual in the summer of 1789, when the old order was vanishing amid the flare of burning castles, was the very worst training for the young French democracy; for it accentuated the egotism of the time, which needed to be kept under restraint. In the absence of the old authority, the only method of preserving order was a sense of civic duty, which would prescribe first and foremost a feeling of regard for the common weal, a conviction that the new democratic system must be based on the loyalty and self-restraint of the masses. Some deputies (e. g. the Abbé Grégoire and Camus) realized this all-important truth. Mounier's committee on the constitution proposed an article (coming just after the definition of Rights) which thus defined duty: "The duty of everyone consists in respecting the rights of others." But the Assembly struck out this article and also another phrase binding them to prescribe the Duties of Man. A motion of Camus to that effect was defeated on August 4 by 570 votes to 433. One member went so far as to say that the duties of man spring naturally from his rights—a disastrous blunder, which was to cost France dear.[1] Its result was seen in the rampant individualism of the following months, when politics degenerated into a game of grab and the Revolution into a tug-of-war between hostile parties. The tendencies towards anarchy were quickened; and seeing that anarchy leads, sooner or later, to a military despotism, Mazzini scarcely exaggerated when he summed up the dynamics of the time in this suggestive formula: "The French Revolution, having begun

[1] *Hist. parlementaire de la Rev. française*, II, 177, 222.

with a Declaration of the Rights of Man, could end only in a man, Napoleon."

The French Revolution, running in this vicious circle, fatally prejudiced the success of the democratic experiment. Mazzini maintained that it merely closed an old era, the era of individualism, and did not initiate the new era, the era of collective energies inspired by duty. This, then, was to be the mission of Italy. Looking back over her annals, blood-stained but ennobled by the unceasing self-sacrifice of her best sons, he believed that so much suffering must lead to a noble consummation. Community in suffering had weakened the old local feelings: the glory of dying for *la patria* had aroused generous feelings which would banish political egotism. Italy, therefore, was the chosen land of the future; and from Rome would sound forth the gospel of duty which Paris had stifled. This is the essence of Mazzini's faith—no blind instinct, but a belief based on knowledge of the past. France had lost her opportunity. England was a land of timid compromise. From Italy, when fully aroused, would come the life-giving message, that all the peoples were bound together by the sacred tie of duty towards Humanity.

Mazzini believed that this inspiring ideal would widen the outlook of Italian patriots. They must be true patriots in order to deaden petty local jealousies. But they would not cast the slough of provincialism in order to encase themselves in the mail of patriotism. The idea of duty must reign in the national sphere. The Italian Republic of the future must consult, not its own interests primarily, but those of all nations, an ideal which would finally sterilize national rivalries. Or, as he developed the theme in his *Duties of Man* (1858), family duty saves a man from being hide-bound in egotism; the national idea ought to exorcize merely family or clan selfishness; while duty to mankind will raise national patriotism on to that higher level where wars of aggrandizement become impossible. As he pithily phrased it: "You are *men* before you are *citizens* or *fathers*." [1]

On the other hand, he reminded those who sneered at patriotism, and put their trust only in cosmopolitanism, that theirs was a futile creed. How can you attain to the vague and vast ideal of Humanity unless you have midway some intermediate form of association? How can individuals, as mere units, move the world? Of course, the thing is impossible save to a handful of idealists. The masses must have something tangible to work on. To take a parallel case. The nation can effectively exist only where men are first banded together in towns and counties. Because narrow-minded people cannot see beyond their town or county, you do not therefore abolish the organization of the town or county. You retain that organization and seek to widen their outlook, so that the Yorkshireman or the Devonshire-man may attain to the nobler pride of being an Englishman. During long ages tribe fought with tribe, county with county, then Scots with English. But the tendency, though painfully slow, is sure, which endows men with the wider vision; and then these local strifes of Irish and English, Venetians and Genoese, Lombards and Tuscans, seem absurd. They die of themselves because men have gained the broader view, and use these local sentiments as means of attaining to a higher level than would be possible if they sought to reach it by a single bound. The cosmopolitan, who sneers at his country and raves about Humanity, is like a man who disdains the use of stairs and seeks to leap to the first floor. Such efforts have always failed. To ignore the tremendous force of nationality, and grasp at a vague cosmopolitanism by means of groups and unions, is to bridge the torrent by gossamer, as recent events have shown. No! The true line of advance is, not to sneer at nationality and decry patriotism, but to try to

[1] Mazzini, *Duties of Man* [Everyman edit.], ch. 5.

utilize those elemental forces by imparting to them a true
aim, instead of the false aim which has deluged Europe with
blood.

No part of Mazzini's teaching is sounder than that which
deals with the necessity of recognizing the patriotic instinct
as fundamental to human nature, and also of educating and
directing it to nobler ends than those to which it has so often
been perverted. To the Italian workingmen, some of whom
were running after cosmopolitan will-o'-the-wisps, he gave
this wise advice: "Do not be led away by the idea of improving your material conditions without first solving the national question. You cannot do it." And again: "In laboring, according to true principles, for our country we are
laboring for Humanity. Our country is the fulcrum of the
lever which we have to wield for the common good. If we
give up this fulcrum, we run the risk of becoming useless both
to our country and to Humanity." [1]

On the question of assuring political unity to his divided
and oppressed countrymen, Mazzini accepted no compromise. He would not hear of a federalized Italy, vegetating
under the shadow of the Vatican. On the surface that
scheme of Gioberti (outlined above) seemed easy to realize;
and in 1846, when the reforming Pope Pius IX was elected, its
chances seemed roseate. Gioberti appealed to history and
tradition as proving that Italians needed a large measure of
freedom of action in local affairs; and he summed up his contention in these impressive words: "To suppose that Italy,
divided as she has been for many centuries, can peacefully
submit to the rule of one man is mere folly. To desire that it
should come about by violent means is a crime."

Well! The folly has been committed. The crime has
been perpetrated. The impossible has come to pass. Thanks
to the fiery zeal kindled by Mazzini; thanks also to the sword

[1] Mazzini, *Duties of Man*, pp. 54, 55.

of Victor Emmanuel, the diplomacy of Cavour, and the self-sacrificing heroism of Garibaldi, Italy is united, though not in the form of a Republic. The causes of the failure of the Republic do not concern us here. The ideal of Mazzini was unattainable, but not because the Italians rejected it. On the contrary, they rallied to it enthusiastically and in large numbers. In the early half of 1849, when Mazzini was the leading Triumvir of the Roman Republic, with Garibaldi as virtual commander of the troops; when also brave Manin and the Venetians kept the banner of the Republic flying against the shot and shell of Austria, there was some ground for hoping that the cause of Young Italy would survive. All depended on the action of the young French Republic; and if that Government had granted the support which Mazzini at first expected, France and Italy might have expelled Austria's white coats, as they did ten years later. The fate of Young Italy was sealed when the French Republic (or rather its President, Louis Napoleon) attacked the Roman Republic, while Austria wore down the defenders of Venice. The Italian Republic was crushed by foreign intervention; and the Judas of the time was Louis Napoleon.

Nevertheless, though Young Italy lay crushed in the summer of 1849; though Mazzini and Garibaldi barely escaped with their lives; though French bayonets supported the Pope at the Vatican, and the white coats of Austria terrorized the North, Italy did not die. She lay stunned and bleeding under the heels of the autocrats, Napoleon III and Francis Joseph. But she had caught life-giving words that were more potent than the bayonet and the gibbet. Garibaldi had shown that her sons could fight on equal terms with the best troops in Europe. The "honest King," Victor Emmanuel, was a centre of hope; and his Minister, Cavour, sought by all possible means to remedy the disasters of 1849 by pitting France against Austria. He succeeded; and the

Italian monarchy of to-day is largely the outcome of his masterly statecraft. Even Cavour and Victor Emmanuel, however, would not have succeeded but for the faith and enthusiasm kindled by Mazzini. Men who are nerved by a conviction of the justice and beneficence of their cause are not daunted by one or two disasters. As Mazzini wrote after the surrender of Rome to the French: "What was failure to men who were imbued with our beliefs?"

That faith was rooted more deeply than in a merely national patriotism. The men of Young Italy shed their blood, not merely that their country might gain the unity she so much needed, but in order to assure her civilizing mission to mankind at large. They caught a vision of other peoples freed and regenerated. In words which are prophetic, if not for his day, then perhaps for ours, Mazzini thus outlined the future: "The map of Europe will be remade. The countries of the peoples will arise, defined by the voice of the free, upon the ruins of the countries of kings and privileged castes. Between these countries there will be harmony and brotherhood. . . . Then each of you, strong in the affections and aid of many millions of men speaking the same language and educated in the same historic tradition, may hope by your personal effort to benefit the whole of Humanity."

Yes: the map of Europe is now to be remade. The remaking can proceed on two methods; either on force or on a sense of duty; either on the military results and the calculations deduced therefrom, or according to the dictates of justice and enlightened common sense. If the peace of the year 1916 or 1917 be merely the law of the strongest, expressed in terms of their actual losses and hoped-for gains, it will be the parent of future wars. If, however, the settlement be dictated by a deep sense of public duty both towards the present and future generations, then the future may prove to be that which the prophetic eye of Mazzini discerned.

LECTURE VI

THE AWAKENING OF THE SLAVS

THERE is a homely saying, "It takes all kinds of people to make the world." And this, which is said of individuals, is equally true of the peoples. The richness of the life of Europe is due mainly to the variety of its races and to their strong individuality. Their competition in the spheres of thought and action, even their collisions in war, are healthier than the stagnation produced by the dead uniformity of the life of pre-reform China. Even to-day, surely, it is true:

"Better fifty years of Europe than a cycle of Cathay."

To dash off the characteristics of the European peoples would lead merely to smart epigrams, and I will not attempt it. It is impossible to assess correctly the peculiarities even of the subdivisions of the great family which we are now attempting to study. But there is a general likeness about all the Slavs, especially those who still remain in the great plain of East Europe.

Those wind-swept steppes, where winter fastens a relentless grip for five months and then breaks into a brief spring and an almost torrid summer, beget extremes of character. The long and bitter cold fosters the virtues of toughness and endurance, also of firm comradeship. For the millions of Russian peasants life is a stern struggle, and only by holding stoutly together in their Mir, or village commune, have they survived. The drought of summer is equally to be dreaded. A prey, therefore, to extremes of climate, the peasant develops a tenacity unequalled except among races

that struggle against the sea; and there is in the landsman of
the East more of resignation and melancholy than is found
among the seamen of the West. When the Muscovite has
fought on to the very end and knows he is beaten, he lies
down and dies with the fatalism of the Asiatic. The Slavs,
essentially an emotional people, have been moulded by this
life of extremes. Both they, their literature, and their music
are intense and passionate; but an undertone of melancholy
pervades even their outbursts and their excesses. It is the
grund-motiv of the Russian winter.

Their great enemy of peace time is also their best friend
in war time. From the dawn of history in the days of Herodo-
tus the dwellers in the great plains have, with the aid of this
fearsome ally, worsted all invaders. Darius, the Tartars,
the Poles, Charles XII of Sweden, Napoleon (shall I add
Hindenburg?) recoiled, shattered. On the other hand, the
plain-dwellers have been remarkable for a certain want of
enterprise in war. In campaigns far from home they have
rarely been formidable, except against Turks and Tartars.
Russia, while strong for defence, is weak for offence. She
resembles Antæus rather than Hercules. Her people and her
Government lack the resourcefulness, foresight, and organizing capacity needful for the success of distant expeditions.
Professor Brandes goes so far as to say: "Passivity shows
itself in their public and private life, in the submission to the
powers that be. . . . Though the Russians are a brave and
a remarkably steadfast people in war, they are the most
peaceful and unwarlike people in the world." [1]

This is a little exaggerated; for Russian Tsars have given
rein to warlike ambitions; and their people have followed
them; but the people themselves cling to their homes, to
their creed, and to the old ways. From the time when the
Greek colonists of the North Euxine gazed with terror on the

[1] G. Brandes, *Impressions of Russia*, p. 26.

Scythian tribes moving about in their quaint caravans, those barbarians were far less formidable than they appeared. Only when pressed from the East, in the Dark Ages, did they or their successors send forth swarms that overran Europe. Considering her vast bulk, Russia has played a curiously small part in European history. Her natural trend was towards Asia rather than Central Europe; and she rarely moved westwards except after attacks from the west.

The first event that thoroughly aroused her from Oriental torpor was the invasion of Napoleon in 1812. Untaught by his failure to break down the resistance of the Spaniards, he strove to wear them out in the South-West and the Muscovites in the North-East, though in both cases he confronted an enraged people, unconquerable if only they would persevere. The life of Russia was widespread, impalpable, scattered through myriads of villages, each of which, thanks to the Mir, was a self-sufficing unit. So soon as these units were resolutely of one mind, the only thing left for the invader was—to decamp.

Among the many perversities of that curious book, *Power and Liberty*, Tolstoi hit upon an undoubted truth, that Napoleon's Grand Army had to leave Moscow because the peasants burnt their corn and fodder rather than let the French have it. The triumph was essentially a national triumph; and the spirit of the Russian troops led even single individuals to attack the French during the long retreat. In a military sense, the Russian pursuit was often tardy and ineffective; but General Winter did his work thoroughly; and the Russian people have never lost the feeling of pride in that overthrow of the great Emperor. It was in Spain and Russia that he encountered forces beyond even his power, the strength of a truly national resistance.

As in Spain, however, the new patriotism was soon diverted into reactionary paths. The Tsar, Alexander I, drifted away from the Liberalism of his youth; and, worst of all, he did not keep troth with the Poles. That gifted people had done and suffered much for Napoleon; and in 1814-5 Alexander held out to them the hope of a national kingdom under his suzerainty. The autonomous Kingdom of Poland soon vanished, and Alexander's suzerainty became a despotism. Since then there has been no real union of sentiment between Poles and Russians, and the latent hostility of the Poles to Russia is, perhaps, the chief of the weaknesses of that Empire. That huge organism has never been thoroughly unified. It is an agglomerate, in which the Great Russians of the North and North Centre predominate; but their hard and practical nature consorts ill with the more sensitive Little Russians of the South, the Poles of the West, and the Finns of the North-West. Whether these peoples will ever cordially unite is one of the problems of the future. Certainly, the autocracy has failed to unite them. Perhaps this war, and after the war, democracy, will accomplish the feat. Russian enthusiasts are confident that democracy will succeed where despotism has failed. In this respect the development of Russia presents a signal contrast to that of Prussia and Germany, which has been vitally connected with the House of Hohenzollern. That House has unified the German people, and, since unification, has drilled them with Prussian rigor. Whatever be the faults of the Tsardom, it has not cast all the Russians into the same mould; but perhaps the failure to unify them results from the lack of cohesion which has always marked the Slav peoples. They have attained to a racial feeling, but not to the wider feeling which may be termed national.

The centrifugal tendencies of the Slavs of the Austrian Empire are also very marked. Limiting our attention here to the South Slavs, we notice that the awakening of their national sentiment somewhat preceded that of the Russians. Nature and the current of events had alike been unfavorable to the South Slavs. Their furthest off-shoots on the South-West had settled in the mountainous country a little to the North-East and East of the Adriatic. Those living north of Trieste and around Laybach are termed Slovenes; those further East are Croats; those to the South-East, Serbs. The Slovenes are almost completely cut off from the Adriatic by a thin but tough belt of Italians around Trieste; and the Croats and Serbs, who stretch as far as that sea, have long been severed from it politically by the Venetian Republic and by its heir, Austria. Those Powers kept a tight hold on the coast line and rigorously subjected the Slavonic population. It has never been Italianized, still less Austrianized. These Slavs, cut off from effective use of the sea, and divided between Hapsburg, Venetian, and Ottoman rule, remained in a state of torpor until about the time of the French Revolution, when the blows dealt by the Republican armies to Venice and Austria awakened the Slovenes and Croats. Already the latter had resisted the attempts of the Magyars to denationalize them. In the Hungarian Diet the proud *nobiles* began to use the Magyar tongue instead of Latin. The Croat deputies resisted; and in 1805 the Bishop of Agram advocated the use of the Slavonic tongue in public speech and documents. Thus the national sentiment of the South Slavs was first excited by Magyar aggressions at the expense of their mother-tongue.

Next, the blows of Napoleon fell on the House of Hapsburg. After Austerlitz he compelled Austria to cede East Venetia, Istria, and part of Dalmatia to his new Kingdom of Italy. After the campaign of Wagram, he forced her to give up the lands which he styled the Illyrian Provinces, and they formed part of the French Empire during the years 1809–13. Marshal Marmont, the new Governor, introduced the *Code Napoléon* and many of the benefits of the French administration. The effects were very marked. These

South Slavs, previously divided and misgoverned, now entered into a large and generous polity. The French encouraged the official use of the Slovene and Croat languages, which had previously been proscribed; and a new national feeling was aroused by newspapers and books written in the vernacular. Such was the gratitude of these downtrodden peoples to the French Emperor that the poet Vodnik sang his praises in an ode, entitled *Risen Illyria:* "Napoleon has said 'Awake: arise, Illyria.' She wakes, she sighs—'Who recalls me to the light? O great hero, is it thou who wakest me? Thou reachest to me thy mighty hand; thou liftest me up.' . . . 'Resting one hand on Gaul, I give the other to Greece that I may save her. At the head of Greece is Corinth; in the centre of Europe is Illyria. Corinth is called the eye of Greece. Illyria shall be the jewel of the whole world.'" On the fall of Napoleon, the Slovenes again reverted to Austria, and the Croats to Hungary. Again the Magyars began their attempts to Magyarize, but encountered an equally obstinate resistance, the Croat and Serb provinces declaring their equality of rights with the Hungarian. They were sister provinces, not daughter provinces.[1]

When part of an oppressed people gains the boon of self-expression it is natural that the other part, which is still gagged, should struggle ceaselessly. Already the Serbs had striven valiantly against Turkish tyranny. They never despaired of casting off their vassalage to the infidel; for deep in their hearts was the memory of the glorious days of King Dushan, who, about 1350, ruled over all the lands from Philippopolis to Agram, and southwards as far as Corinth. Serbia was then the most powerful State of South-East Europe, and owned ports on the Ægean and Adriatic. At the capital, Uskub, Dushan held a splendid Court, Greeks, Bulgars,

[1] Léger, *Austria-Hungary*, p. 440: Seton-Watson, *The Southern Slav Question*, pp. 25–9.

even the proud Magyars bowing before Serb supremacy. This promising civilization fell at one blow. The Turks burst upon it and levelled it to the ground at the Battle of Kossovo (1389). A legend, preserved ever since in ballad form, tells how the fate of Serbia and of Christendom was decided by the treachery of a Serb chieftain, Vuk Branko-vich, who, at the crisis of the struggle, rode over to the infidels with 12,000 panoplied horsemen. Whether true or not, that story struck deep into the hearts of the Serbs. During five centuries of slavery the exploits of Dushan and Milosh were handed down by minstrels (*gosslari*), who secretly assembled the peasants and sang to them of the great days when Serbs gave the law to Bulgar and Greek, and fell beneath the Mos-lem yoke only because of treachery within the fold. Thus a consciousness of superiority lingered on, inspiring the belief that, if ever they had a chance, they would beat back the in-fidel to Asia and renew the ancient glories of Uskub. A people that cherishes those historic memories can never be alto-gether enslaved. The fire of patriotism, though choked down, will smoulder on; and a spark may bring it to a flame.

That spark, as we have seen, was blown eastwards from Italy and Croatia. The exploits of Napoleon and the fall of Venice and Austria sent a thrill through the Slavonic world; and the Serbs challenged the supremacy of the Turks. At that time the Ottoman Empire was rent asunder by revolts of local pashas and of that privileged military caste, the Janissaries. The Serb peasants therefore won many suc-cesses; and the invasion of Turkey by the Russians in 1809 promised for a time to lead to the expulsion of the Turks from Europe. In 1812 the Russians had to withdraw in order to meet Napoleon's Grand Army; but, as formerly in 1791, they had spread far and wide the hope that the great Slav brother would free his "little brothers," the Roumans, Bulgars, and Serbs. By the treaty of 1812 Russia wrested from the Turks the boon of autonomy for the Roumans, together with certain privileges for the Serbs. These last were soon revoked by the ever faithless Turks, who sought to cow the Serbs by impaling or brutal floggings. They failed. An enterprising Serb peasant, Milosh Obrenovich, proclaimed a general rising on Palm Sunday, 1815, worsted the enemy and extorted the right to bear arms.

In the sequel the Ottomans might, perhaps, have overwhelmed the Serbs but for the risings of the Greeks, the revolts of the Janissaries, and the Russian invasion of 1829. The rapid advance of the Russians as far as Adrianople spread dismay among the Turks; and Sultan Mahmud II made peace with Russia, conceding among other things further rights to the Serbs. Thus a second time Russia befriended the Slavs of the Balkans, and they (the Bulgars included) acknowledged her as their champion. In 1842 Serbia (now enlarged) refashioned her popular Assembly, so that what had been merely a mass meeting of warriors became an organized representative body. Thus the Serbs were the first of the lesser Slav peoples to develop constitutional rule, albeit of a very crude and primitive type. This fact is far more significant than the sanguinary strifes between the rival Houses of Karageorge and Obrenovich. Those struggles, culminating in the murder of King Alexander in 1903, are relics of a barbarous past; but they have not very seriously retarded the progress of the people at large. That progress is what really matters; and the acts by which a community of peasants step by step won its freedom from the warlike Turks and then gradually attained to self-government bespeak not only tenacious bravery, but also a political capacity of no mean order. In the nineteenth century nationalism which is limited solely to military exploits counts for little. As Napoleon once remarked, the civilian is a wider man than a mere warrior, because "the method of the soldier is to act despotically; that of the civilian is to submit to discussion, truth, and reason." Similarly, a people which excels in the affairs of peace must in the long run surpass one which, like the Turks, devotes itself almost exclusively to war. In fact, nothing is more remarkable than the manner in which the Christian peoples of the Balkans though often defeated and massacred, have slowly but surely outstripped their Ottoman conquerors and persecutors. It is because the latter have relied upon force, while their subjects have applied the new national enthusiasm to all sides of the widening life of to-day. The futility of relying merely upon armed might nowhere appears more clearly than in the changed relations of the Turks and their victims.

The fortunes of those subject peoples, however, depended largely upon their champion, Russia. In that Empire, especially at the old capital, Moscow, pride of race has always been strong. If Petrograd was, as its founder claimed, the eye by which Russia looked out on Europe, Moscow was the eye of faith, which discerned in Muscovy the means of national uplifting. There are always two currents of thought in Russia, the cosmopolitan, strong at Petrograd, which has tended to rely on Germany and France; the other, all-powerful at Moscow, which circles about things Muscovite, and claims that they alone will save Russia. The former party tend to depreciate Slavonic customs and sometimes vent their despair in such an outburst as that of Turgenieff: "What have we Russians invented but the knout?" The others, strong in faith and contemptuous of foreign ways, retort: "Yes: whenever it rains at Paris, you put up your umbrellas at Petersburg." The men of faith point out that in 1812 the might of Napoleon collapsed before the patriotic endurance of Russian peasants; and in that time of trial the nation proved its capacity both to save itself and save Europe. Away, then, with servile imitation of the foreigner!

Away with the German customs and notions imported by Peter the Great and Catharine!

Such was the creed of a group of students at the University of Moscow. They sought "to found an independent national culture on the basis of popular conceptions and Byzantine orthodoxy, forsaken since the time of Peter the Great."[1] In the main they relied on the Mir and the communal customs connected with it; also on the Greek Church as the true exponent of Christian tradition. They forswore the use of French and German in favor of the hitherto despised vernacular. At first, i. e. early in the thirties, the movement had no political significance; but Nicholas I soon used it to further his reactionary policy; and the tendency of a narrow nationalism to play into the hands of a despot was illustrated in Russia more promptly and banefully than perhaps anywhere else. Thanks to the Slavophiles of Moscow, Nicholas was able to subject the teaching of philosophy to the clergy of the Greek Church and that of history to the supervision of the public censor. Foreign books and newspapers were as far as possible excluded; and Russia entered upon the path of political and religious reaction.

A similar degradation befell a somewhat cognate movement. Panslavism can boast a revolutionary origin. It was first proclaimed at Paris by a Russian, Bakunin, who is also the father of Nihilism. A Russian student, he sat at the feet of Hegel at Berlin, and finally settled in the French capital, where he associated with many Polish exiles. At a banquet, held in 1847 to commemorate the Polish rising of 1830, he spoke passionately in favor of a federative union of all Slavs. Such a scheme implied the grouping together, not only of the Russians and Poles, but of the Checs and Slovaks of Bohemia and Moravia, and of the South Slavs oppressed by Austria and Turkey. As a revolutionary pro-

[1] *Russia before and after the War*, p. 138.

gramme this scheme of Bakunin surpassed all the political schemes of the nineteenth century. Its complete realization would involve the destruction, not only of Austria and Turkey, but also of the Empire of the Tsars; for, as was said by Herzen, one of the Russian revolutionaries: "When we win Constantinople, then the iron sceptre of Peter the Great must break; for it cannot be lengthened to reach to the Dardanelles."[1] The Russian anarchists, then, hoped by arousing a Slavonic enthusiasm among all branches of that widely scattered race to break up three great Empires and spread revolution far and wide. In its origin Panslavism was rather an anarchic than a merely national movement. In this respect it contrasts with the Pangerman movement, which has always been intensely national.

Panslavism, however, gradually shed its revolutionary slough and became almost a conservative force. The steps by which this came about are obscure; and we need merely note that in the critical years 1875–7 Panslavists and Slavophiles tended to merge. Both sections sought to force the Tsar, Alexander II, to draw the sword against Turkey; and, despite his clinging to peace, they prevailed. In the period of reaction which set in under Alexander III Panslavism and the Slavophile movement proper were the twin steeds yoked to the autocrat's car. Both proved to be equally amenable to the yoke; and the reactionary Ministers of Petrograd succeeded so skilfully in manipulating Panslavism that wags have wittily dubbed it "the romanticism of red tape." The phrase crystallizes the tendencies of the Slavs towards emotionalism in politics, which, in practice, inclines them towards submission to the powers that be in Church and State.

Another weakness of the Slavs is their wide dispersion. The Germans and Magyars thrust a solid mass between the

[1] *Ibid.*, p. 308.

North and South Slavs of the Austrian Empire; so that, even
in the cataclysm of 1848-9, the two halves of that people
failed to unite. For all their eager fraternizing in a great
Slavonic Congress at Prague in the spring of 1848,[1] the South
Slavs soon ranged themselves on the side of the Hapsburgs
and helped to re-establish that dynasty. It is curious that
those years witnessed the rise both of the Panslavonic and
Pangerman ideas, the former at Prague, the latter at the
German Parliament assembled at Frankfurt; but nothing
came of either of them. Democracy and nationality then
hindered each other, and found no support from any powerful
State. Their ignominious collapse subjected those formative
ideas two decades later to the domination of *Realpolitik;* of
Gortchakoff in Russia, of Bismarck in Prussia.

Not that the call which in 1875 came to Russia from the
Slavs of the Turkish Empire was devoid of romance; for, if
ever cause was lofty and holy, it was that which the Tsar,
Alexander II, championed in the ensuing years. But the
Slav movement was finally to suffer from the bargaining and
the statecraft which accompanied and closed those liberating
efforts. Assuredly, the cries which came from Bosnians,
Serbs, and Bulgars were such as no patriotic Russian could
hear unmoved. Bulgaria had lagged far behind her neighbors in developing the national idea, a fact which we may
explain partly by her semi-Slavonic origin. The Bulgars
are akin to the Magyars and Turks. True, after their long
stay in Russia, near the Volga, they were Slavized and finally
became Christian. But their stolid and unemotional temperament still proclaims their affinity to the Turanian stock;
so that persons who lay stress on mere questions of race and

---

[1] The Committee's manifesto contained these words: "After centuries
of misery we have at last become aware of our unity, our responsibility
for one another." But the proceedings at the Congress demonstrated
the extreme difficulty of common action.

ignore the higher and more lasting influences making for nationality may perhaps find some slight excuse for the recent treachery of the Bulgars to the Slavonic cause. But let it ever be remembered that the Bulgars owe everything to the Slavs. Besides, of themselves they would never have shaken off the Turkish yoke. In 1834 Kinglake travelled from Belgrade through Sofia to Constantinople. In Serbia he recognized the people as Serbs. East of the Dragoman Pass, that is in Bulgaria, he deemed all the inhabitants Turks, except a substratum of Christina rayahs unworthy of his notice. It was reserved for the French professor of Slavonic literature, Cyprien Robert, to unearth the Bulgars, and he found them secretly cherishing their religion, customs, and language, all of them not very unlike those of the Serbs.

Apart from a few local risings of Bulgar peasants, goaded to madness by Turkish tyranny, nothing of importance occurred in their history until 1870, when they gained the right to have their own religious community, that is, apart from the Patriarch of the Greek Church. The Porte was induced to take this step, partly by the demands of Russia, France, and Great Britain, who always favored Bulgarian claims; partly also because it hoped by this means to divide the Christians and weaken them. Far from that, the formation of a national Church strengthened the Bulgarian movement at the expense both of Greeks and Serbs. To the new Church were allotted Bulgaria Proper, also the vilayets of Adrianople, Salonica, Kossovo, and Monastir. In these districts, which Serbs and Greeks also claimed, the Bulgars soon began a vigorous propaganda by means of churches and schools, which soon withdrew vast numbers from the Greek Church. Sir Charles Eliot believes that this act halved the numbers of those who previously were counted Greeks.[1] The Bulgars also stole a march on the Serbs in the districts of Kossovo

---

[1] Sir C. Eliot, *Turkey in Europe*, pp. 259, 291.

and Monastir. A Serb gentleman once informed me that his people never suffered a worse blow than the allocation of Old Serbia to the Bulgarian Church. The consequence was the growth of an intense rivalry between Bulgar, Greek, and Serb, especially for supremacy in Macedonia. The present war is in large measure the outcome of the racial jealousies which the Porte kindled, or rather rekindled, by its firman of 1870. Bulgaria is making a mad bid for the conquest of the territory which the Porte gave to her ecclesiastically in 1870. It was not until late in the nineteenth century that the Serbs gained the right to open their schools in the vilayets of Monastir and Salonica: and not until 1900 did they acquire a national church.

In this respect Serbia has been very unfortunate, while Bulgaria enjoyed exceptional good fortune. Ever since 1805 the Serbs were struggling for their independence from the Turks. Yet in 1870 at one bound the Bulgars passed them by in the race for supremacy, which depends largely on religious organization. How much this meant was seen in the racial statistics of Macedonia; in which the priest and schoolmaster were able to make what they liked of that doubtful material. The report of a Russian victory, a lavish distribution of Austrian gold, or fear of the incursion of a robberband of Greeks sufficed to make the wretched peasantry of Macedonia turn over from one side to the other with unblushing effrontery.

To revert to the events of 1875; the reopening of the Eastern Question certainly came from the Serbs of Bosnia and Herzegovina. Their revolt in the autumn of 1875 was caused by the exceptional cruelty of the Turkish tax-gatherers after a bad harvest. That rising has by some been ascribed to Austrian agitators. But when crops were seized wholesale, and the sanctities of home were foully outraged, what need is there to drag in the foreign agitator? The explanation is not supported by the facts of the case, and it is, in general, a singularly superficial way of accounting for a widespread movement.

Last of all the Slavonic peoples, the Bulgars began to stir, but in the partial way that might be expected from their canny and suspicious nature. An ambitious Bulgar youth, named Stambuloff, who had been educated in Russia but expelled thence as a revolutionary, came back to Bulgaria in 1875 and sought in mid-September to raise the peasants against Turkish tyranny. Of the thousands who promised to help him only thirty assembled at the rendezvous near Eskizagra. These courageous men fled to the Balkans. Thence Stambuloff and a very few escaped to Russia, where once again he sought to rouse his sluggish countrymen.

He had grounds for hope. The men of Herzegovina and Bosnia held out on the mountains, despite the hardships of the winter of 1875-6. The efforts of the three Empires (Austria, Russia, and Germany) to induce the Sultan to grant effective reforms were thwarted by the British Cabinet. Lord Beaconsfield, unwarned by the utter failure of our Crimean War policy, refused to support the efforts of the three Empires to apply pacific coercion in order to extort from Turkey the needed reforms. The British Ministry went further. It sent our Mediterranean squadron to Besika Bay, near the entrance of the Dardanelles, a step which encouraged the Sublime Porte to expect the armed succor of Britain in case of war with Russia. These events increased the excitement both of Moslems and Christians in the Peninsula. Serbia could scarcely keep her sword in its scabbard; and the Bulgars hoped for armed aid from Russia. A Bulgar schoolmaster found out a curious anagram. The Bulgarian letters which make up the words "Turkey will fall," when put in the form of an addition sum (letters serve as figures in the Cyrillic alphabet) amount to the total 1876.

The news whetted the eagerness of the peasants. The Bulgarian novelist, Vazoff, in his romance, *Under the Yoke*, has described the secret preparations for the revolt. The women worked hard to bake quantities of biscuit for the men who were to take to the hills at the end of April, 1876. The men made guns, pikes, knives; while the more ambitious of them, who had heard tell of what the Carlists did long before in Spain, cut down their finest cherry trees, hollowed them out, hooped them with iron clamps, and hoped for great things from these curios mounted on the hills. Imagine the sequel on the first of May, when the Turkish Bashi-bazouks marched in. No deafening roar, no devastating volleys of grape shot on the Moslems; only a dull puff, a sound of rent wood, and the gunners themselves laid low. That pathetic incident was typical of the whole rising. With the narrow view of things, which is characteristic of the Bulgars, some villages waited for the others to begin; and most never began at all. On the few bolder spirits the Turks burst like a whirlwind; and then the work of murder and outrage began. At Batak the Moslems, after accepting the surrender of the place, drove the men into the great church and set it on fire. Out of seven thousand inhabitants five thousand were done to death.

But the victims did not die wholly in vain. When these horrors became known in England they aroused a storm of indignation against Turkish misrule. Mr. Gladstone voiced that indignation in tones which rang through the world. Even to-day, or certainly up to their last mad plunge, the Bulgars reverenced his memory and kept his portrait in their cottages beside that of "the Tsar Liberator."

For Alexander II now listened to the fervid demands of his people for armed intervention. Gallant little Serbia had drawn the sword against the Turks; and the sight of the Serbs struggling against great odds stirred Slav opinion to its depths. As before, Slav sentiment centred at Moscow, while official circles at Petrograd and the Tsar himself, suspecting that crusading fervor concealed revolutionary designs, sought to turn the people from their purpose. In this they failed. Finally, after curbing Slavophile sentiment for a year, the Tsar perceived that further delay would unite the naturally conservative Slavophiles with the Nihilists; and when the Sublime Porte, still trusting to British succor, refused all offers of compromise, he declared war on Turkey. The ensuing struggle was fertile in surprises. Even with the help of Roumania, Russia barely overcame the Turks at Plevna, and then had to submit her first terms of peace, those of San Stefano, to the arbitrament of Europe. Owing to the opposition of England and Austria, a far less drastic settlement of the racial questions of the Balkans was arrived at in the Treaty of Berlin (July, 1878). That treaty cut down the new Bulgarian State, from the San Stefano limits, which would have brought it near to Salonica, and penned Bulgaria Proper up in the province north of the Balkans. The Bulgars there were divided from their brethren south of that chain so as to weaken that people, whom British and Austrian statesmen hastily assumed to be the puppets of Russia. The gratitude of the Bulgars to Russia, however, vanished when the new Tsar, Alexander III, proceeded to treat them as puppets. His harsh overbearing ways alienated them; and on their declaring for the union of the two Bulgarias in 1885, it was England, under Lord Salisbury, which favored the union, while the Tsar, chiefly from hatred of the Bulgarian prince, Alexander, opposed that most natural and salutary step. The statesmanlike policy of Lord Salisbury had been prompted largely by our ambassador, Sir William White, a warm friend of the Christians of the Balkans; and thus the evil effects of Beaconsfield's pro-Turkish and anti-national policy were reversed.

We must postpone to a later lecture a consideration of Balkan politics in the sequel. I have sought to bring before you a succession of scenes in which the Slavonic peoples struggled for self-expression and for the most part utterly failed. During many years Panslavism was a name that aroused terror in the clubs and salons of London. The reality never alarmed those who observed the centrifugal tendencies always potent among the Slavs. Hitherto Panslavism has been a political Tower of Babel.

LECTURE VII

THE GERMAN THEORY OF THE STATE

"The aim of the State is not dominion or the restraining of men by and the subjecting of them to a foreign yoke. On the contrary, its aim is to deliver each man from fear so that he may be able to live with the utmost possible security. . . . The aim of the State is liberty."—SPINOZA, *Theological Politics*, ch. 20.

AT the beginning of this lecture I wish to make it clear that my aim is, not to discourse upon any one theory of the State, but rather to show how the notions about the State, now prevalent in Prussia and Germany, developed there. I will also not waste time by seeking to frame an elaborate definition of the term "State." The word itself means that which is fixed or established, that is, in regard to law and government. Setting aside minor differences, there are three chief conceptions regarding the State. The first regards it as depending on the will of the monarch (e. g. *l'Etat c'est moi*, of Louis XIV); or, secondly, of a privileged set of persons; or, thirdly, of the mass of the people. The organism which gives effect to one or other of those wills is the State. Notions respecting it are always changing; and amidst the present cataclysm he would be a bold man who would ascribe definiteness and fixity to the conception of the State.[1] But the desire for something approaching to definiteness, if not fixity, is inherent in the human mind, witness the declaration of poor, bewildered Louis XVI not

[1] I accept the description given by Mr. C. Delisle Burns [*The Morality of Nations*, p. 28] as "the sovereign organization for the attainment of common political good."

long before the French Revolution. Conscious that *le régime
du bon plaisir* (i. e. of the King's will) was doomed, he declared that France desired *une manière fixe d'être gouvernée*.
That admission heralded the dawn of a democratic order on
the Continent. Thenceforth the typical State was not to be
the expression of one man's will, but of "the general will,"
which Rousseau affirmed to be the source of all law and
administration.

But even when we limit ourselves to the modern State
based on representative institutions, we find a great variety
of conceptions regarding its functions. The most important
of these differences arise respecting the claims which the
State may make on the liberty and services of the individual
citizen. Here at once we plunge into the region of contro-
versies that are certain to become more and more acute.
In this connection it is well to remember that the democratic
States of the Ancient World, e. g. that of Athens, required
implicit and almost unlimited obedience from their citizens.
These were bound in many ways which we should deem
abhorrent to true liberty. Transport a Londoner to the
Sparta of Lycurgus, and he would protest vigorously that
he was a mere bondman, not much better off than the actual
slaves. Again, the fact that a Roman citizen could for
heinous crimes be degraded to the position of a slave illus-
trates the radical difference between the authority of the
State over the individual in the Ancient and Modern World.
The power of the Greek or Roman State was far greater than
we should allow; yet that power was accepted as in the natural order of things by citizens who considered themselves
entirely free.

When, therefore, we approach the subject of the authority
of the modern State over its citizens, we must remember
that all well-educated men were familiar with a condition
of society in which a democratic State could demand nearly

everything from its subjects. Lord Acton well describes the
State in ancient times as being "both Church and State" in
one.[1] It was even more. It was Church and State and an
exacting employer all in one.

Lord Acton's simile is even more applicable to the absolute
monarchies of Western Europe; for their authority was based
on a theocratic creed as well as on military force. Henry
VIII, Philip IV, and Louis XIV claimed to exercise an authority conferred by divine power and sacred unction. This
was the theory adopted by the Hohenzollerns in the year
1701. The claim in their case was singular; for everyone who
looked on at the gaudy ceremony of coronation of the first
Prussian King at Königsberg was aware that the royal title
was gained by hard bargaining with the Hapsburg Court at
Vienna. Nevertheless, Frederick I of Prussia decided that he
would be a king by the grace of God, and he did his utmost
to get himself taken seriously in that character. He crowned
himself, as all his successors have done, excepting the greatest
of them. Frederick the Great deemed that ceremony a
farce, besides wasting money better spent on troops or road-
making.

By this resolve he struck the key-note of Prussian policy.
Nothing for show, everything for efficiency. Rigorous
efficiency in all departments of government, such was the
aim of Frederick II. Nothing was too small to escape his
ken. In time of peace he visited once a year every part of
his kingdom. He decided what marshes should be drained,
or what rivers embanked for the prevention of floods. It
was his fostering care that improved the woollen trade,
founded new villages, and sought to construct a navy and
plant colonies overseas. He was his own commander-in-
chief, foreign minister, chief engineer, and chief development commissioner. Woe betide the official who neglected

[1] Acton, *History of Freedom and other Essays*, p. 16.

his work! Frederick's eye was sure to detect the fault and punish it severely. During one of his journeys he happened to find out that a courier was kept waiting owing to the somnolence of a postmaster. The King rushed upstairs into the offender's bedroom, dragged him from bed, and administered a severe caning under the most favorable conditions.

Frederick II was the Prussian State. To his nephew he described his feelings early in the reign as he surveyed the splendid troops and full coffers bequeathed by his fathers. He spent some of the money and increased the troops. Then he looked around him and saw four provinces that he might seize. He chose Silesia. "Therefore" (he wrote to his successor), "have money, give an air of superiority to your troops. Wait for opportunities, and you will be certain, not merely to preserve, but to increase your dominions. . . . All depends on circumstances and on the courage of him who takes." Such are the fundamental maxims of Prussian statecraft: "Be strong, be ready, then make your *coup*."

But if Frederick schemed and tricked, it was for Prussia; and it was for Prussia that he was ready to bleed and die. His letter, of October, 1760, written in the midst of a seemingly hopeless campaign, strikes a high note: "I regard death from the Stoic point of view. Never shall I see the moment that forces me to make a disadvantageous peace. No persuasion, no eloquence, shall ever induce me to sign my dishonor. . . . Finish this campaign I certainly will, resolved to dare all, and to make the most desperate attempts, either to succeed or to find a glorious end."—That is the spirit which prevails over less determined foes, whose chatter about peace proclaims their half-heartedness, or at least their lack of the supreme resolve of the hero. It is this rigorous spirit, rigorous towards self as well as towards others, which has made Prussia so formidable. Rightly to understand the Prussian idea of the State, you must first understand historically the Hohenzollern spirit; for it is that spirit which has made the State. The State is merely the machine; that spirit is the inner fire which imparts to the machine its terrible force; and that spirit is still in its essence the relentless but also self-sacrificing energy of Frederick the Great.

The extent to which the personality of her rulers affected the administration of Prussia is obvious from a glance at her fortunes. Frederick the Great raised her to the rank of a Great Power. But, as Mirabeau pointed out in 1786, that position was very precarious. Under the rule of his vicious, extravagant, and vacillating nephew, Frederick William II, Prussia sank quickly to the second rank. The weakness and pedantry of his son, Federick William III, completed her misfortunes. But a change came over the scene in the years 1807-13. The people, formerly passive in the hands of their rulers, became keenly interested in the revival of their State. Schiller and Fichte had awakened a truly national German feeling; and the reforms of the Prussian statesmen, Stein, Scharnhorst, and Hardenberg, in those years made Berlin the one possible centre of political union for all Germans. The Prussian people were identified with the Prussian State, as was the case nowhere else in Germany; and Germans elsewhere looked to Prussia to save them from Napoleon. It was the energy of thinkers and men of action at Berlin that expelled the French and made Prussia the leader of Germany. Depressed by the weaknesses of Frederick William IV, she was raised to unexampled glory by William I and his paladins; and in 1871 she unified Germany.

Now, Prussia was the same State, yet that State varied enormously according to the human element. Therefore it is fallacious to suppose that there is some magic in the Prussian State, or in the German Empire founded on it.

To theorize about the Prussian State as though it were everything in the developemnt of Prussia and Germany is absurd. The rulers and statesmen are more important than the State. Indeed, from the time of the Great Elector down to Wilhelm II it is they who have made or unmade the State.

Nevertheless, the development of ideas about the Prussian State deserves careful study. Though that polity made unheard of demands on the citizens, yet it looked after their interests with almost grandfatherly care. Bismarck, on introducing the first measures that were to be known as State Socialism, declared that they formed no new departure; for the House of Hohenzollern had always governed with a view to the welfare of the poor. This was certainly true of its best members. For instance, Frederick the Great, in 1766, refused to countenance a proposal of one of his officials to tax fat cattle when imported. "A crown a head on the import of fat cattle? Tax on butcher's meat? (he exclaimed). No. That would fall on the poorer classes. To that I must say no. I am, by office, procurator of the poor (*avocat du pauvre*)." The Hohenzollerns have generally sought to consult the welfare of their poorer subjects; and this was the reason why German provinces, like Silesia, which were annexed to the Prussian monarchy, soon became Prussian. That kingdom was not liked—it never has been —but its vigorous rule promoted prosperity and pushed the people on. By these qualities many able Germans were attracted to Berlin. Of the men who helped to raise up Prussia after the terrible overthrow of 1806–7, the most illustrious were non-Prussians. Stein was a Franconian, Hardenberg and Scharnhorst were Hanoverians, Queen Louisa and Blücher were Mecklenburgers, Fichte and Gneisenau were Saxons, etc.[1] Scarcely a single able leader was a Prussian.

[1] Seeley, *Stein*, II, 403.

Yet the best brains in Germany gravitated to Berlin. What was the attractive force? Not mere ambition; but rather the conviction that there alone worked an efficient machine.

These considerations explain why practically all German theories as to the State originated in Prussia. Omitting the French and freedom-loving theories of William von Humboldt, the first is that of Kant, the idealist of Königsberg. Sir John Seeley said that Kant's severe gospel of duty was a natural outcome of the age and the polity of Frederick the Great. It may even be affirmed that Kant's teaching about the State is an idealization of all that was best in the actions of the great King. Kant seeks to repress the selfishness of individuals, and to compel them to work for the general weal. They must do so (he claims) in the interest of order; for order is essentially the aim of the State; and order can be assured only by submission of individual whims to the will of the community. True; for the purpose of securing order, the State must be endowed with force; but it does not exist for the sake of developing force. (There Kant is far ahead of the latest school of German thinkers.) The *raison d'être* of the State is order.

On the outbreak of the French Revolution, liberty, progress, and peace become the dominant aims of Kant. They are set forth in his essay, *Perpetual Peace* (1795), which remains a landmark of the generous cosmopolitanism that was soon to be submerged by the Napoleonic deluge. We shall return to Kant's Essay in Lecture X.

The next of Germany's thinkers was a Saxon by birth. Fichte (1762–1814) spent most of his early life in Saxony, Switzerland, and at Jena; but a charge of infidelity drove him from his professorship at that University; and in his thirty-seventh year he settled at Berlin, where he found more toleration and freedom of speech than in the smaller centres. In 1800 he published an Essay, *The Exclusive*

Commercial State, in which he advocated rigorous protection and an almost socialistic ordering of all activities. The work glorified the rigorous tendencies of Prussian politics; and may be termed a rather viewy precursor of the State Socialism of Lassalle and Bismarck.

Far fuller and more philosophical were Fichte's lectures on "The Characteristics of the Present Age" (1804)—at which we glanced in Lecture III. In them he eulogized Prussia. In the tenth lecture he rejected a theory of the State, which describes it as merely a juridical institution, i. e. concerned with the making and administering of law. Such a conception might do for Saxony or Würtemberg; but it appeared to him inadequate amidst the varied activities of Prussia. He put forward one which certainly did not err on that side. He called the absolute (i. e. complete or perfect) State "an artistic institution, intended to direct all individual powers towards the life of the race and to transfuse them therein." In previous lectures he had explained his sense of the importance of the universal life, declaring that the aim of mankind was, or should be, " to order all their relations with freedom according to reason." Human life, then, ought to be concerned with reasonable activities, which must enjoy a reasonable amount of freedom. As for the State, it would be the means of furthering the higher aims of mankind. It would restrain the selfishness of individuals by directing their energies towards the welfare of the whole of Society. Fichte's aim, at this time, was cosmopolitan, not Prussian.

But his methods were autocratic. As the collective activities of mankind do not in the least degree attract the numerous individuals to whom the triumph of reason is naught and the pursuit of their own unreason is everything, he maintains that they must be compelled to enter into the collective life. Seeing that they "feel no desire, but, on the contrary, a reluctance, to offer up their individual life for the race," there must be some power which will compel them, if need be, to die for the community. That power is the State.

Fichte's words describing the State as an artistic institution are somewhat odd, seeing that it directs all individual powers towards the life of the race. But he explains that by "artistic" he means that which raises men above their natural level so as to fulfil the destinies of the race.[1] The State carries out this purpose and compels all citizens, without a single exception, to dedicate themselves to this duty. Even the rulers are subject to this obligation. It is their directing power and the directed energies of the governed, which together make up the State. He proceeds to make another claim: "All individual power which is known and accessible to the State is necessary to it for the furtherance of its purpose: its purpose is *Kultur* (civilization); and in order to maintain the position to which a State has already attained, and to advance still further, it requires at all times the exertion of every available power; for, only through the united power of ALL, has it attained this position. Should it not take the Whole into account, it must needs recede, instead of advancing, and lose its position in the ranks of civilization."

These statements call for some explanation. Fichte spoke at a time when the Government of Prussia was in the weak and nerveless hands of Frederick William III; when, also, Germany was sinking under the control of Napoleon and accepted his direction in the spoliation of the Ecclesiastical States and knightly domains. In view of that disgraceful scramble Fichte desired to strengthen Prussia; he sought also to remind her King and nobles that the State had declined in authority and prestige since the days of Frederick

---

[1] I think that the phrase "a civilizing institution" comes nearer to Fichte's real thought.

the Great. Then the Prussian State was the embodiment
of power. In 1804 it was not; and unless it recurred to the
forceful ideals of the earlier generation Prussia must degenerate. Fichte therefore sought to press every faculty of the
Prussian people into the public service; and he clinched his
demand by this declaration: "In a perfect State no just
individual purpose can exist, which is not included in the
purposes of the community, and for the attainment of which
the community does not provide." Or, to translate it into
modern parlance: "Every activity of life belongs to the
State; and the perfect community will have a place for
every man and will see that he fills that place to the utmost
of his power."

Obviously, Fichte was heading towards a drastic State
Socialism. He did not use the term "Socialism," which,
indeed, does not first appear until some thirty-two years
later. Still less did he see his Spartan ideals realized. But
his system would have imposed on Prussia a polity as absolute as that of the Pharaohs, a régime in which individual
liberty would vanish and all the activities of life would be
regulated as they are in an ants' nest. "The general will"
of Rousseau, having passed through the mill of German
philosophical method, came out as the Prussian State, thus
outlined by Fichte.

For the attainment of its complete and characteristic
growth one more element was necessary—that of Nationality.
In 1804-5 Fichte had not yet hit upon that formative idea.
Perhaps he derived it from Schiller's *Wilhelm Tell*, which
seems to have influenced Fichte's *Addresses to the German
Nation*. Or else, as I ventured to suggest, the fall of the
Prussian State after Jena (1806) revealed to him the German
nation. In the earlier lectures on the State he never mentions the nation. He conceives the Christian European
peoples as being very much alike and concerned with the

same purposes. It is the States that are in perpetual conflict, some rising, some falling, according to the degrees of energy and ability which they display; and their true aim is to further the progress of the race as a whole. To take a concrete instance, Prussia and Austria are in constant competition, sometimes in actual conflict. Their rivalry calls forth the powers of their rulers and subjects. Prussia wins because she is the better organized; and her triumph, being a survival of the fittest, furthers the progress of the human race. Fichte was not then thinking of the German race; for indeed it was in so divided and discordant a condition that you could not discern it as a political unit.

By the winter of 1807–8 the way was cleared, and Fichte's *Addresses to the German Nation* called to action, not hidebound States, but a half-strangled people. As always happens in time of crisis, he sought to revive their courage by recalling the mighty deeds that Germans had accomplished both in war and in the peaceful arts—their inventions, commercial development, and learning. He claimed the Reformation as a truly German assertion of liberty of thought; and he vaunted the superiority of the pure Germans over the Franks and other Teutons that had unlearnt their mother-tongue. The nation was now the dominant thought. It eclipsed the idea of the State, as appeared in this passage (Lecture VIII): "Nation and Fatherland in this sense as bearers of and security for earthly immortality . . . far transcend the State in the usual sense of the term. . . . The State only aims at security of rights, internal peace. All that is only the means, the condition, the preparation, for that which patriotism essentially aims at, the blossoming of the eternal and divine in the world." He then asserted that patriotism must direct the State, individual liberty being restricted within as narrow limits as possible. In his earlier notions the State was supreme in order by competition with other States to advance the welfare of the human race as a whole. In 1807-8 he reduced the State merely to a piece of mechanism, driven onwards by the nation, with patriotism as the directing agency. The union of his earlier Pharaoh-like theory with his later claim of the supremacy of the nation prepared the way for the later theory of the German State, conterminous with the German nation, and both impelling, and impelled by, that nation.

His teaching bore fruit in many directions. As the State or the nation requires all the activities of its citizens, it follows that all distinctions of privilege must vanish; for the unprivileged (e. g. the serfs) cannot develop their full powers. The serfs therefore become freeholders; national education begins, so does municipal government, in which men are compelled to take up their duties. All these changes aim at the increase of power and efficiency. For this same purpose compulsion is laid upon them to defend their country. That duty had been required of all Frenchmen of military age by the French Republic in 1793, and more systematically in 1798. After the Peace of Tilsit (1807), Prussia extended the principle of compulsory service to all her sons. Scharnhorst and Gneisenau, the chief designers of the new Prussian army, demanded in the preamble to their reforms that the army must be "the union of all the moral and physical energies of the nation." The phrase recalls the words of Fichte; and it well summarizes the aims of the Prussian patriots of that time. The realization of their ideal in the glorious efforts of the War of Liberation reveals the potentialities of the Prussian State. Dowered with the toughness of the Frederician régime, it is strengthened and enriched by the doctrines of civic self-sacrifice proclaimed by Kant and Fichte.

Long after the fall of Napoleon, the memory of the events of 1813-5 inspired the thinkers of Prussia and Germany.

The energy and order prevalent at Berlin attracted thither many thinkers who began life in the small States. That had happened to Fichte, and in 1818 it happened to Hegel, his successor in the chair of philosophy in that University. Earlier in his career Hegel (1770–1831) had been an enthusiastic admirer of Napoleon and viewed the overthrow of Prussia with supreme indifference; for he saw in the French people and their Emperor the outcrop of the world-spirit. But in his Berlin period he became Prussian. In his lectures delivered there in 1820 he delivered his theory of the State in regard to law. His conclusion was that the State was in the moral order what Nature was in the physical order. As the State sustained and regulated everything, it formed the chief necessity of life for civilized men, and became, in effect, the realized ethical ideal or ethical spirit.

By these claims Hegel raised the State to a supernatural level. There it existed as something perfect, absolute, and superhuman, yet dominating the fortunes of mankind. Apparently, the Hegelian State could not develop or change; for development implies advance from a less perfect condition to one that is more perfect. Hegel also made no allowance for its permeation by the ideals of other States.[1] His ideal creation remains alone, like some Zeppelin tethered a mile or so above Berlin, and dominating earth, air, and heaven itself. Indeed, this simile is too weak to express the absolute self-sufficiency of the Hegelian State. Its creator scoffed at all inquiries as to its origin; for it had always existed while the nation existed. All that he will say on this head is that the State is the outcome of the deep-seated principle of order.[2] This it is which determines the exercise of what Rousseau termed "the general will."

Here at last we come to firm ground; but we remember

[1] See D. Burns, *op. cit.*, pp. 45, 53.
[2] Hegel, *Philosophy of Light*, transl. by S. W. Dyde, pp. 240–65.

that forty years earlier Kant had affirmed the *raison d'être* of the State to be the craving for order. In this respect, then, the Hegelian notion links itself on to the doctrines of Rousseau and Kant; but the outcome is a terrifying and sterilizing creation, whose chief practical duty is to protect "the life, property, and free-will (!) of every person, simply in so far as he does not injure the life, property, and free-will of any other." But, he proceeds, the State is far more than a magnified police officer. The perfect State is a spiritual and all-pervading entity. It is not something separate from each of its subjects. It is not distinct from you, from me. We form part of it; and in this consciousness lies our political freedom. Here we must remember that Hegel admits that a bad State is finite and worldly. But wherein the perfect State consists and wherein a State is bad is not clearly defined.

It may seem impertinent in a mere historian to criticize Hegel; but I cannot avoid the suspicion that, in identifying the subjects with a perfect State, he is confusing the State with the nation. My insular imagination fails to conceive so complete an identification of the citizen with the most perfect State as to become merged into it. That merging is possible in the case of the nation; and I believe that it can be affirmed of every true patriot at a great crisis. Certainly every Briton who now dies for his country makes that supreme surrender on behalf of the nation, or for His Majesty as typifying the nation. Professor Edward Meyer in a recent work claims that it is the great defect of our public life that we do not think about the State. He says: "The Briton never speaks of his State—a State does not exist for him. He either speaks of the Empire or he speaks of the Government, meaning the Government which then handles the rudder of State. A State high above the clash of parties does not exist for the Briton as it exists for the German":

and to this he attributes our political helplessness in this war. Events, of course, will decide that point;[1] and I question whether the average German is filled with much enthusiasm for the German State. I believe that he fights and dies for *das Vaterland*, which is a far more human and inspiring conception than that of the State. The idea of the State, I believe, appeals chiefly to the intellectuals; for, ever since Hegel's day, it has supplied them with a *motiv* for theory-weaving.

However, the question whether a soldier fights and dies for his nation or his State is academic trifling; and (to return to Hegel) I believe that he ascribed to the State much that Fichte had ascribed to the nation. It seems to me that on this topic Fichte's view was sounder. The nation it was which fired France with hope and enthusiasm. The Germans defiantly retorted with their national idea in 1813; and though the idea of the German nation did not in that age find visible expression in a national State, yet there was the chance that it would one day embody itself. To idealize the State in 1830 was surely doubtful psychology and false as history. The criticism of some of Hegel's contemporaries crystallized in the joke that he mistook the Kingdom of Prussia for the Kingdom of Heaven.[2]

Hegel even affirms that the State is the nation's spirit. That again is a question of words; and I cannot see that such a description of the State advances our knowledge of it. We worldly minded students of history want to know, not what the State is, but *how it works;* how it reconciles the often divergent claims of general order and the liberty of the individual. On these topics Hegel is as silent as Rousseau.

[1] See the suggestive remarks of Rev. J. Oman, *The War and its Issues*, ch. III [Camb. Univ. Press, 1915], as to the difference of British and German ideas of the State.

[2] G. P. Gooch, in *Contemporary Review*, June, 1915.

In fact, Hegel, like Rousseau, seems to believe that in that
ideal entity, the absolute State, there will be no opposition.
We reply that that is unthinkable among a free community;
and our suspicions of the Berlin professor are not lessened
by his assertion that to offer the people a constitution is a
mere whim, seeing that a constitution must grow from the
consciousness of the people. "True!" we English reply;
"that is the best method, the English method; but is that a
sufficient reason for refusing the beginnings of a free government to a less fortunate people?" There is, of course, much
truth in Hegel's further statement, that every nation has
the constitution that suits it and belongs to it; but this
assertion again is liable to abuse, if it implies that no arbitrary Government is ever to be overthrown, because the
people do not deserve a better.[1] In practice, Hegel's theoriz-
ing about the State came to be a defence of paternal and
almost despotic Government. "You have a nearly perfect
State" (said he); "be content with it; identify yourself
with it; you need not wish for anything better." Some of
his friends reproached him with deserting his earlier progressive views; and the charge seems proven.

In his next political work, *The Philosophy of History* (1830),
Hegel implicitly defended the Prussian system, which excluded the populace from the political life of the State: he
also decried the results of the French Revolution; and, as for
the English Reform Bill, he declared that it would destroy
what slight measure of governing capacity still survived in
these islands. Moreover (said he), the typical Englishman
was too insular, too whimsical, to understand real liberty,
and always looked at it from the point of view of his own
home. As for Prussia, despite her exclusion of the citizens
from political affairs, she was on the right track; for she
embodied the principle of reason. She was Protestant, and

[1] Dyde, *op. cit.*, pp. 274-82.

she admitted capable men to all posts.[1] What more could they want?

Notwithstanding this discouraging conclusion, the influence exerted by Hegel was very great. Discredited though he was by the later Liberalism (which found its exponent in Bluntschli [2]), his State-absolutism lived on and helped to reinforce the masterful notions of the Bismarck-Treitschke period. Another Hegelian theory tending in the same direction was that of the World-Spirit visiting and vivifying the great peoples in turn, and, in the fullness of time, the German people. But we must postpone to Lecture X an examination of that theory.

So far we have been considering the German idealists. It has been stated that their political teaching was sound, and that the poison which has crept in was due solely to materialism of thought and to its political resultant, *Realpolitik*.[3] But, as I have tried to show, danger lurked in the teachings of Fichte and Hegel. In their Berlin periods they denied individual liberty and exalted the State to a dangerous pre-eminence, while Hegel's later teachings fostered the growth of Prussian Chauvinism. The following years witnessed the publication of Clausewitz's work *On War*, memorable for its declaration that States were always in a condition of struggle, of which war was only an intenser form. Then, too, appeared that exciting poem, "*Deutschland, Deutschland über alles.*"

The popular outbreaks of 1848–9 in Germany concern us here only because the populace everywhere affirmed the

[1] Hegel [*op. cit.*, p. 437] recognizes a South German nationality, because that people was too mixed to accept Protestantism.

[2] See J. K. Bluntschli, *The Theory of the State* [Eng. edit. (2nd), Oxford, 1892]; especially Bk. II for suggestive remarks on the State and Nationality.

[3] Prof. J. H. Muirhead, *German Philosophy in Relation to the War*, Lects. I, II.

supremacy of the whole nation; and when Frederick William IV for a time surrendered to his "dear Berliners" and declared that thenceforth Prussia would merge herself in Germany, the triumph of the nation over the Prussian State seemed assured. Owing to the inexperience and reckless enthusiasms of the first German Parliament, which met at Frankfurt in 1848, all went awry. The old political mechanism was set up again; and, when Germany achieved her union in 1870–1, it was through the House of Hohenzollern and the Prussian State. Consequently, the failures of German Liberalism in 1848–9 have profoundly affected the trend of political thought. Idealism, democracy, and voluntary methods being discredited, the tendency was towards the precepts and practice of Frederick the Great. In short, the age became ripe for Bismarck's gospel of "blood and iron," the way for which was further facilitated by prosperity, and the development of a materialistic philosophy.[1] Bismarck often gibed at the professors and barristers of 1848; but it was their viewiness which prepared the way for his statecraft. The excesses of democrats have always been the best help of reactionaries.

The first sign of the new spirit was an essay by Rouchau on *Realpolitik*. Published in 1853, when the reaction was in full swing, it trumpeted forth the new political materialism. "The State is Power"—such is its thesis. It attracted a far more important man than Rochau, Heinrich von Treitschke, who afterwards developed that theory to its logical conclusion. Treitschke (1834–96) came of a Slav family and was endowed with Slavonic intensity and vehemence, which he vented against that race with all the acerbity of a renegade. His father was a Saxon officer of proved loyalty and steadfastness; but the youth soon displayed far other tendencies. For his first recorded speech,

[1] See Professor Muirhead, *op. cit.*, Lect. III.

delivered at a prize-giving, he chose as his subject praise
of Prussia's championship of German unity; and that incident
is typical as illustrating his natural bent towards Prussianism.
As a student, he read with ardor the *Politics* of Aristotle and
the *Prince* of Machiavelli, dangerous reading for a youth of
his ardent temperament. The study of Fichte and Hegel
fortified his conviction of the need for the supremacy of the
State; and in 1861 (the year of the consummation of Italian
unity) he set forth the ideal of "the nationally exclusive
State," i. e. a State composed of one people. "For (said he)
where the living and indubitable consciousness of unity pervades all the members of the State, there and there only is the
State what its nature requires that it should be, a nation
possessing organic unity." He prophesied that the great
peoples would everywhere form national States—a singularly
correct forecast. In common with all nationalists he detested the House of Hapsburg as artificially clamping together
diverse elements which Nature meant to exist separately.
What, then, would he have said about the Hohenzollern-
Hapsburg-Bulgar-Turkish compacts for the domination of
neighboring lands? Probably he would have defended that
strange league on the ground that the State is power and must
hew its way through to more favorable positions on the North
Sea and in the Levant; but assuredly such a plea would
contradict his earlier contention, that the State must be
conterminous with the nation, and that it is well even "to
amputate alien elements of the population." [1]

His eager nationalism led him to advocate the absorption
of the smaller German States by Prussia; and indeed he
invited her to attack them. The end, said he, would justify
the means; and they would soon benefit by her vigorous
rule. Such was his plea in 1864. He knew perfectly well

[1] Treitschke overlooked the Poles of Posen, then, as now, utterly un-
Prussianized.

that the King and Bismarck were then governing illegally and despotically. All the same, he prayed that they might succeed; for Prussia alone could unify Germany. She alone could win the coveted duchies, Schleswig-Holstein, and thereby assure to Germany a commanding position in the North Sea and the Baltic. Similar reasons induced him to side against Austria and her South German allies in the struggle of 1866. After the triumph of Prussia, he, a Saxon by birth, demanded that she should annex Saxony outright, for the crime of taking the side of Austria; and he professed to be surprised and pained that his father should speak of him as "a political Jesuit."

Treitschke persisted in his claim that Prussia should lead the German people forward to power and prosperity far beyond the bounds of the nation. In a remarkable passage in his essay *Bundesstaat und Einheitsstaat* he pleaded for an effective unity of Germans so that they might be able to compete with other peoples for the commerce of the oceans. The South Sea was calling for traders; and mighty united nations were pressing in, while the Germans could only follow humbly at a distance their more fortunate predecessors. Why should Germans be steeped in inland notions? Let them hear the call of the sea and organize themselves fitly for a great future. That future they could realize only by means of political unity. Enough of their old federalism! What they needed was unity—an *Einheitsstaat* (a united State).

This was the thought that impelled his angry demand for the annexation of Saxony, as well as Hanover and Hesse Cassel. In August, 1870, even before Napoleon III was overthrown at Sedan, Treitschke passionately demanded the annexation of Alsace-Lorraine. That the people of those provinces objected to such a change was nought to him. "These provinces (he cries) are ours by the right of the sword;

and we will rule them in virtue of a higher right; in virtue of the right of the German nation to prevent the permanent estrangement of her lost children from the Germanic Empire. We Germans, who know both Germany and France, know better what is for the good of the Alsatians than do those unhappy people themselves, who, in the perverse conditions of a French existence, have been denied any true knowledge of modern Germany. We desire, even against their will, to restore them to themselves." Then comes the naïve and illuminating admission: "We are by no means rich enough to renounce so precious a possession." He also expressed the hope that the extension of the responsibilities of the German people would lift their politics above doctrinaire pettiness "to a great, strenuous and positive conduct of the affairs of the State."[1]

This last statement is instructive, in view of the opposition already offered by German Liberals and Socialists to the annexation of Alsace-Lorraine. The progressive elements in Germany deprecated such an act,[2] not only from principle, but also from expediency; from principle, because the transfer of people like cattle to an alien rule was abhorrent to democracy; from expediency, because the Government of these unwilling subjects must be more or less coercive; and coercion renders the Government harsher towards its own subjects, besides furthering the growth of militarism. Now, it was precisely for these reasons that Treitschke advocated the annexation. He wanted to have done with idealism in order to assure "a positive conduct of the affairs of the State," in other words, he aimed at the triumph of *Realpolitik*. Bismarck was of the same mind as Treitschke. The Iron Chancellor, speaking to Busch just after Sedan, laughed at the notion that Germany would annex Alsace in order to re-

---

[1] H. W. C. Davis, *The Political Thought of Treitschke*, p. 112.
[2] Busch, *Bismarck in the Franco-German War*, I, 147.

teutonize her lost children. All that talk was merely the vaporing of German professors (not yet in favor): "It is the fortresses of Metz and Strassburg which we want, and which we will take."

That is the essence of *Realpolitik*. Germany needs Metz and Strassburg for military reasons. Therefore she will annex them. True, a little later, Bismarck wavered about annexing the wholly French population of Metz; but the German Staff never wavered. They had their way, and that way led towards a more drastic polity. Thus, just as Frederick II's persistent rigor resulted from his deliberate choice of an aggressive and therefore militarist policy, so, too, the aggrandized Germany of 1871 imposed on Europe the evils of an armed peace and on herself a more absolutist régime.

In proportion as the aims of Berlin politicians became more and more objective, so did the teaching of Treitschke. He laughed at a political science based on abstract principles, viz., the science of Kant, Fichte, Hegel. He claimed that it must be the outcome of the experience of each people. As the peoples differed widely in character and local conditions, so, too, must their polity. To affirm the necessary superiority of any one State-system was ridiculous. The nation must construct its own form of polity in order that it might lead its own life. The true guide was history, not the doctrine of abstract right; for history showed what the people was and what it wanted. So far, good. Few Englishmen will dispute these dicta. But Treitschke proceeded to claim that in matters political there was no positive right and wrong. Every nation must construct its own moral code—as the Germans have done.

His reasoning at this point is illogical; for, though he postulated the complete supremacy of the State in secular affairs, he deliberately excepted matters of conscience which (said he) pertained to the relations between God and man, and were beyond the cognizance of the State. Yet the State must form its own code of morality. The only escape from the difficulty is to claim that State morality is something entirely separate from the morality of the individual. That is what the followers of Treitschke have both affirmed in their lecture-rooms and practiced in Belgium.

Finally we may note that Treitschke identified the State and the nation. He defined the State as a people united by legal ties to form an independent power. On this subject again his ideas were inconsistent. Sometimes he denied that the State was an organism and declared it to be a person (presumably the nation personified). Elsewhere, however, he thus defined it: "The State is the public power for defensive and offensive purposes." (That is, it is a magnified drill-sergeant.) Pursuing this trend of thought, he thus narrowed down the functions of the State: "It only represents the nation from the point of view of power" (a political Hercules). But, again, he said: "The State is the basis of all national life" (an eternized Frederick the Great).[1]

It is difficult to frame any intelligible theory out of these descriptions; and the composite photograph made up from these personifications would be an odd creature, recognizable only by the spiked helmet. But there is one feature common to them all. They body forth the idea of power; they imply a something which functions with tremendous energy, which belongs more to the barracks and the workshop than to the Church and the University. Treitschke's State, whatever he may at times say to the contrary, is a mechanical contrivance designed for conquest; and to this contrivance the German people is closely linked.

These conceptions of the State as drill-sergeant and of the populace as recruits mark a serious set back from the ideas

[1] Treitschke, *Politik*, I, pp. 28-32, 62-3; quoted by H. W. C. Davis, *op. cit.*, pp. 127-131.

of Fichte; for he insisted on the ideal character of the nation. In his view the nation far transcended the State, which concerned itself with government and law. The nation looked to higher things, to the blossoming of the eternal and divine in the world. Despite his too hopeful idealism, Fichte was far nearer to the truth than Treitschke. For, surely, the State is the organism, while the nation is the brain and the soul. True, the nation needs the State to endow it with hands and feet. But the nation remains the directing agency vitalizing and directing the body politic. Indeed, the nation survives, even when all the machinery of Government is shattered. At this very time the Belgian State and the Serbian State scarcely exist; but the Belgian nation and the Serb nation endure—aye, and will endure; for their sublime courage has endowed them with immortality. This is what German politicians and German professors cannot understand. Destroy all the machinery of government and you have destroyed the nation, say Treitschke and his successors. Possibly it is, in part, these mechanical notions which have led them astray into their recent adventures; for otherwise their conduct is altogether inexplicable. It becomes dimly intelligible when compared with that of Napoleon, who, carrying eighteenth-century materialism into the realm of high policy, deemed the Spanish nation conquered when he had beaten their armies and seized the machinery of government. It is the nemesis of a forceful régime that it neglects everything which cannot be measured in battalions, money, and foot-pounds.

Treitschke had before him the example, not only of Napoleon's disastrous blunder, but also that of two peoples who defied all assessment by official measures. During a century (with a short interval after Waterloo) the Poles enjoyed no political existence. Yet have the Poles ever ceased to be a nation? The other instance is even more striking. During

1800 years the Jews have had no State. Nevertheless, Jewish nationality is one of the powerful influences of the world, often seemingly destroyed, but ever rising again in Phœnix-like vitality. In spite of these patent proofs of the superiority of the nation to the State, Treitschke and his many followers insist upon degrading the nation, which is essentially a spiritual entity, to the level of the organism which merely endows it with power for action. I believe that there is no hope for German political thought until it frees itself from this disastrous confusion. "Back to Fichte" ought to be the cry of all German idealists; for, though his political creed contained much that was despotic, yet he proclaimed the all-important truth (veiled to Treitschke), that a nation exists in the realm of spirit and cannot be made or unmade by force. When that discovery is brought home to the German people they will have taken the first step towards a political renascence. Then they will liberate themselves from the traditions of Frederick the Great. Then they will reorganize themselves on rational lines, free from the overmastering influence of the Prussian State.

LECTURE VIII

NATIONALITY AND MILITARISM

OUR studies in national movements have been by no means complete. We have passed by the struggles of the Poles, Belgians, Greeks, and Hungarians, also the efforts of the French for a revival of their polity in the critical years 1871–5. The study of the French *Risorgimento* reveals the sterling worth of that people and also the practical usefulness of patriotism in rebuilding an almost shattered society. No better guide and inspiration can be found for the tremendous work of reconstruction which awaits the European peoples at the close of this disastrous war.[1]

We have also had to omit from our survey the most surprising of all national movements in our age, that of Japan. A genuinely patriotic impulse it was which suddenly transformed Japan from a mediæval into a modern State, which absorbed much of the best in European civilization without impairing the strength of the old Japanese chivalry (*Bushido*). Finally it was a keen sense of national honor which flung back Russia from Korea, expelled Germany from Shang Tung, and is now loyally helping the Allies by furnishing Russia with the munitions of war. All this has been done by a people which less than half a century ago fought with bows and arrows and frightened the enemy with masks. It is a romance; and the soul of the romance is the intense

[1] The revival of France in 1871–5 will form one of the "special periods" for the Historical Tripos of 1917, etc.; and will be dealt with by members of the Cambridge History School.

patriotism which nerves the Japanese, from the highest
to the lowest, with devotion to the Mikado as the embodiment of all that is holy and lofty in the national life. There
is terrible poverty in Japan; but no Japanese would dream
of whining: "I have no country to fight for."

These great movements one and all demonstrate the tremendous force of Nationality. It may be granted that
that feeling appeared long ago in England, France, and
Spain; yet its influence was fitful by comparison with that
which it has recently exerted upon the European peoples;
and I think we may ascribe its development largely to the
spread of education and of facilities for trade and travel.
In the Ancient and Mediæval Worlds the town or even the
village was the typical social unit. By degrees that unit
enlarged. In times of general danger men recognized their
kinship with men previously deemed strangers or enemies;
and with the widening of social intercourse that conception
acquired strength until it flashed forth in a universal consciousness at a time of mental exaltation such as that which
exhilarated France in 1789–90. Elsewhere, as in Spain, England, and North Germany, danger of conquest by the foreigner furnished the mental stimulus; and then what had
been a group-consciousness, a county or provincial feeling,
became a permanently national feeling. As I have tried to
show in these lectures, this widening outlook, this pride in
the country instead of merely in the county, opens up an
immense store of vital energy. There passes through those
diverse groups and classes a thrill which makes them one
body politic—not a *corpus vile* on which Kings and lawgivers
may work their will, but a conscious powerful entity which
bends them to its will. Such is the change which has come
over the peoples. It has refashioned the map of Europe,
forming in the centre massive blocks out of what was a
feudal mosaic, dissolving the Ottoman Empire into its com-

ponent racial groups, in short, giving political expression to the settlements of the peoples effected during the Dark Ages.

Reverting to our political bioscope of Lecture I, we see that the political boundaries of Europe now correspond nearly to the more permanent of the conquests made by the barbarian invaders who shattered the Roman Empire. First there was imperial unity, which gave way before tribal chaos; then there ensued long and painful jostlings; then an assorting process under monarchs; then there emerged groups of tribes nearly related, which developed at the expense of merely traditional or enforced groupings; finally there were formed the solid homogeneous blocks of to-day. Obviously, here we have an elemental force of incalculable potency, whether for good or harm. The reasonable method of regarding this national instinct is, not to sneer at it as something old-fashioned and certain soon to disappear before an enlightened cosmopolitanism, but rather to try and understand it, so as to dissociate its baser elements from those which may further the progress of mankind.

Firstly, then, what is Nationality, using the term in its abstract sense? [1] Perhaps we shall come nearer to the truth if we apply the method of exclusion and discover what it is not. Our studies have, I believe, led us to doubt whether it is determined by race. Let us consider this question in the light of the science of ethnology. We now know that the old notions about "the European family" and its supposed division into Celts, Teutons, etc., are without scientific foundation. There is no European family, no Celtic race, no Teutonic race. Anthropologists, by their careful examinations of certain physical characteristics, such as the shape of the skull and the color of hair and eyes, have proved that so-called racial divisions based on language or tradition are

[1] See the Preface for notes on the terms "people," "nation," "nationality."

not fundamental. Speaking broadly, there are three races in Europe: (1) the tall, fair, long-haired race which spreads from the British Isles and the North of France through Flanders and the North European plain and Scandinavia as far as the Gulf of Finland; (2) the broad-headed race, generally termed the Alpine, which inhabits the greater part of Central France, Central Europe, and the Balkan Peninsula; (3) the Mediterranean race, inhabiting the European lands north of the Mediterranean Sea, with the exception of North Italy and the Balkan Peninsula.[1]

Science, then, knows of no essential physical difference between a North-West German, a Fleming, and a North Frenchman. There is a difference between this northern family and the Central and Southern Germans and Frenchmen. Considered according to race, Germany is tripartite, and so is France. There is no marked distinction of race between a Norman and a Hanoverian; between a Lyonnais and a Bavarian; between a Provençal and a Calabrian. In the French army there are three distinct racial types: so there are in the German army. Yet those three diverse types are welded into political and military entities, which oppose each other with the most desperate determination. But this political and military grouping is not racial; it is based on difference of culture (using the term in its widest sense). Though there is no such thing as a Celtic or Teutonic race, Celtic or Teutonic culture is a reality. So, too, the Anglo-Saxon people is a conglomerate, made up of several racial elements; but Anglo-Saxon culture has marked and distinct characteristics, which, from our present point of view, overshadow the physical differences above noted. It is also important to get rid of the old notion that there is a fundamental

---

[1] The above summary, of course, does not comprise the Jews, Turks, Bulgars, Magyars, and Finns. It is only a very general statement. Deniker subdivides the three races named above into several groups.

physical difference between the average Englishman and the
average North Frenchman, and between him and the average
North German.[1] What differences there are have developed
later. They are due to language, tradition, religion, custom,
and, finally, political grouping and political sentiment. Of
course these differences make up nearly the whole of life to
the modern man; but (to put it baldly) the Englishman is
not a different *animal* from the North German, or he, again,
from the North Frenchman. Science has rendered a great
service by disproving that hoary superstition.

No! Only in a very crude form (like that which now prevails in Germany and the Balkans) does Nationality depend
on race. The Belgian *littérateur*, Laveleye, well expressed
the thought: "In proportion as the culture of a people advances, identity of race and of blood exercises less power on
it, and historic memories exercise more power. Above
ethnical nationalities there are political nationalities, formed
by choice (one may say), rooted in love of liberty, in the cult
of a glorious past, in accord of interests, in similarity of moral
ideas, and of all that forms the intellectual life."[2] Here,
however, I must regretfully remark that this peaceful and
ideal development is apt to be interrupted by inrushes of
sentiment and passion. At such crises, especially during
war, the adage "Blood is thicker than water" holds good;
and the affinities produced by generations of culture vanish
under the drag of racial instincts that seemed to be dead.
Then the cultured European gives place to the tribal warrior.

In normal circumstances, however, Nationality does not
depend on race. Does it, then, depend on language? Here
certainly we come nearer to a powerful political influence.
But again consider. In the French army are Bretons and a
few Basques and Spaniards who speak no French, yet are

[1] W. Z. Ripley, *The Races of Europe*, ch. 6.
[2] E. Laveleye, *Le Gouvernement et la Démocratie* (1891), I, p. 58.

enthusiastically French at heart. In the German army are Wends who in a political sense are thoroughly Germanized, not to speak of Poles, Danes, and Lorrainers who are not Germanized. In the Austrian army are peoples speaking eleven distinct languages; yet there is in that army, as in the Austrian Empire, far more solidarity that was believed to be possible. But the crowning proof that language does not determine Nationality is found in Switzerland. The Swiss comprise portions of three peoples, which speak French, German, and Italian;[1] yet they remain at peace, though over the borders their kith and kin are at war. How is this possible? Merely because language does not determine nationality. The sentiment of Swiss Nationality, rooted in pride in their historic past and in contentment with an almost ideal polity, has triumphed over linguistic differences. Tri-lingual Switzerland remains at peace—agitated, it is true, for language is a powerful tie. Nevertheless, the spiritual union of that people holds firm; and its triumph is an augury of hope for the future. Scarcely less remarkable is the case of the Jews, at which we glanced in Lecture I. They have retained their solidarity, though dispersed during long ages, and divided by sharp differences of language. Only where congregated together in large numbers do they habitually use Hebrew. In Spain and the Balkan States they use Spanish; in Russia and Poland they speak either Polish or a corrupt German; in Morocco, Arabic. Yet they rarely lose their Nationality.[2]

The case of the Swiss and that of the Jews, then, seems to

---

[1] I omit the Romansch, spoken in the Engadine, as too small to count.

[2] Ripley, *op. cit.*, p. 369; S. B. Rohold, *The War and the Jew* (Toronto, 1915), shows that 350,000 Jews are fighting for Russia, 180,000 for Austria, over 15,000 for us, and over 10,000 for France. Yet, though loyally obeying their Governments and fighting against their co-religion-ists, they remain Jews.

show that language is not necessary to, though it may help on, the forming of a nation. Probably, with the spread of education, language will play a smaller part than before. Welsh is dying in several parts of Wales, especially in the industrial districts; and the smaller languages will doubtless vanish, and with them racial differences and jealousies. Migration and emigration help on the assimilating process. In the United States and Canada few languages except English, French, and German have a chance of surviving, and French and German only in certain areas. Speaking generally, in the new lands the smaller languages tend to disappear. Dutch (in a very simplified form) persists in South Africa; but there, too, commerce helps on the more useful language, English. Indeed, the victory of General Botha over Herzog at the polls in South Africa may prove to be the beginning of a genuinely Anglo-Dutch reunion, which will be neither English nor Dutch, but Africander (perhaps bi-lingual for some generations), loyal to the Empire which not only tolerates but fosters within its fold all peoples, all creeds, all languages. The present war has been a terrible set back to the progress of mankind; for it has revived national hatreds and has arrayed against each other peoples speaking different languages; but there are tendencies at work, more permanent than war, which lessen linguistic differences and induce peoples of diverse tongues to live together in friendly union. Of these Federations, Switzerland, the United States, and the British Empire (which is in spirit a Federation rather than an Empire) form the most promising examples; and the present disastrous conflict will probably tend ultimately to strengthen the development of such unions existing independently of race or language. Such at least is the tendency among the leading peoples of the West. They do not need to conquer their neighbors; they attract them by the charm of their culture.

And this, surely, is the type of Nationality which will ultimately prevail over the crude force that is now devastating the world.

No! Nationality does not depend on language. Still less does it depend on a State. As we saw in the last lecture, a nation that depends on a State is mistaking an organism for the life and soul of that organism. In modern times, national feeling has fashioned States, and is always at work refashioning them in accordance with new needs. Nations make States; not States, nations. The one exception is Prussia; so long as she limited herself to the unification of the German people, she achieved remarkable success; but so soon as the Prussian State sought to Germanize other peoples, it utterly failed. Herein, surely, lies one of the chief causes of the deep hostility between the Germans and other peoples. The Germans have glorified the State and have sought to force their *Kultur* on neighboring highly civilized peoples, who resent that process. Even if, by some miracle, they succeeded in this war, their effort would be doomed to failure, as surely as that of Napoleon the Great. For it violates a fundamental conviction of the modern man.

Lastly, is Nationality an emanation of the World-Spirit? Hegel (in his *Philosophy of History*, 1830) put forth a theory which assumed that a world-force visited the peoples in a predetermined order and endowed them with exceptional vitality for some special task. While they performed that task, they were "moral, virtuous, vigorous." Thereafter, they declined, and another took up that or some similar task. The theory finds little support from History. It breaks down in the case of China, which during thousands of years has pursued the even tenor of its way, with few signs of decline, and, indeed, recently with many signs of rejuvenescence. The theory also seeks to account for the decay of the nations, both ancient and modern, on a single hypothesis; whereas history shows that decline and decay were due to very diverse causes, many of them of an agrarian or social character but slightly understood in Hegel's day. Nations also may seem to be on the downward trend, like the France of Louis XV and XVI, and then by a conscious and determined effort of reform they will shoot up again to unimagined heights of power, declining once more when that power is abused by a dictator, Napoleon. If Napoleon was the chief emanation of the World-Spirit, as Hegel long assumed him to be, how came it that he left France far weaker than he found her? Did the World-Spirit suddenly change its mind in 1813 and resolve to desert him and go over to the Allies?

On these and similar topics the World-Spirit theory offers no adequate explanation. Indeed, it cannot explain the complex phenomena of the rise and fall of nations. That certain peoples have now and again displayed marvellously increased vigor is true; but that phenomenon is generally due to one or more of the following causes: There may be a fusing together of various tribes by some able leader or under the impulse of religious fervor (as happened to the Arabs after the time of Mohammed). A great warrior may have incited peoples to wars of ambition. Or, on the other hand, a nation, when threatened with conquest, may be thrown back on itself and develop to the utmost the powers that generally go unused. Or, again, a people can be stimulated by becoming the exponent of some great idea, as were the Swedes of Gustavus Adolphus by Reformation fervor, or the French Revolutionists by the ideas of liberty, equality, and Nationality. Lastly, geographical discoveries and mechanical inventions bring some peoples to the front and depress the fortunes of others, as is evident from the history of Venice, Portugal, Holland, Great Britain. Looking at the causes that make for the rise and fall of nations, we discern a great variety; they range from warlike ambition or the spur of hunger, to impulses of an ideal nature, such as religious zeal, or newly aroused national pride, or wars of liberation. Sometimes a new energy raises the people to a higher level of thought, art, or invention. Again, it drives them to the conquest of new markets. How is it possible to refer to any one cause impulses of so bewildering a variety? Label your *causa causans* "World-Spirit" if you like; but remember that it is a very Proteus, now flashing forth as a warrior, then shrinking into a huckster; now an artist or poet, then a politician; now a philosopher, then an explorer; now an admiral, then a mechanic or engineer. You must run through the whole range of life in order to fill up all the characters that your Spirit may assume.

Lastly, remember that the theory of a World-Spirit inflating one people and deflating others in a predetermined order is morally mischievous. For it tends to puff up with pride a people which believes it detects some sign of the spiritual afflatus; while it also disheartens peoples that deem the deflating process begun, and thereby discourages the timely efforts at reform which can nearly always avert collapse. Believe me, that a fatalistic theory, such as that of the World-Spirit, has little warrant from history. It does not apply to peoples that refuse to bow down to the supposed decrees of fate. Only those peoples are sure to perish who tamely prostrate themselves before those decrees.[1]

We have now cleared the ground of faulty or inadequate explanations of Nationality. Perhaps we shall best understand what it is if we briefly review the events that first made it a force in the modern world.

Recent history is held to begin with the French Revolution of 1789: and Alison classed all the campaigns up to Waterloo under the Revolution. Is it not truer to fact to subdivide the period and say that the first phase of Nationality

[1] I think that Nationality explains several of the cases of exceptional vitality which Hegel ascribed to his World-Spirit.

as distinct from Democracy begins with the Spanish Rising of 1808? It ends with Waterloo. The second phase commences fitfully in 1830 and 1848, and more definitely with the Italian War of Liberation in 1859. From 1859 to the present is pre-eminently the climax of the Age of Nationality. By this I mean that the idea has permeated the masses of the population and has increased their power for action. True, the national idea had previously dawned upon poets and thinkers. It vibrates in the verse of Dante, Chaucer, and Shakespeare; but, as we saw in Lecture I, it did not permeate the masses, except at intense moments of their life, such as coincided with the exploits of Jeanne d'Arc, the repulse of the Spanish Armada, or the revolt of the Dutch "Beggars" against Spain. Subsequently, it died down even in France, England, and Holland; for the Religious Wars divided peoples against themselves, and, on the cessation of those strifes, dynastic wars or the growth of absolutist States half stifled the sentiment. Louis XIV personified the French nation, but so successfully that the nation was but half aware of its own existence.

Much preparatory work had to be done before this discovery was possible. The shipbuilders, road-makers, and traders played their part in bringing men together. Thinkers pointed out what was natural, what artificial, in their society. But when all this preliminary work was ended, and men of different provinces of France began to greet each other instead of scowling, any widespread impulse was certain to produce a new and vital union.

Such an event was the Revolution. It changed the half-animate clods into citizens, but it also sent through them a sympathetic thrill which made the citizens a nation. France is often termed the political laboratory of Europe; for her actions are more striking than are the gradual unfoldings that characterize our annals. Certainly, it is in French history that the development of Nationality is most clearly outlined. The merging of different peoples and diverse provinces in a single monarchy was the work of French monarchs and statesmen, so that, except in a few moments of inspiration, the nation existed only by and in the person of the King. As the monarchy declined under Louis XV and XVI, the nation emerged; and, early in the Revolution (as we saw in Lecture II), the disputes of the National Assembly with the King brought the sense of Nationality to sudden maturity. It found expression during the famous sitting of August 4, 1789, when Lorraine, youngest of the French provinces, expressed her desire to join intimately in the life of "this glorious family."

I know of no words that better describe Nationality. It is an instinct, and cannot be exactly defined; it is the recognition as kinsmen of those who were deemed strangers; it is the apotheosis of family feeling, and begets a resolve never again to separate; it leads to the founding of a polity on a natural basis, independent of a monarch or a State, though not in any sense hostile to them; it is more than a political contract; it is a union of hearts, once made, never unmade. These are the characteristics of Nationality in its highest form—a spiritual conception, unconquerable, indestructible. So soon as clans, tribes, or provinces catch the glow of this wider enthusiasm, they form a nation. And thus it was that France burst into her new life. Her long chrysalis stage, when patriotism clung about the old monarchy, was ended; and the nation stood erect and defiant. England, Italy, Illyria, Spain, Russia, Germany, successively felt the impact of this new vital force, and responded with messages, first of sympathy, then of distrust, finally of hostility. Thus, within twenty-five years, Europe was awake, and became a camp of warring nations.

During the Revolutionary and Napoleonic Age, then, France exhibits Nationality at its best and at its worst. In its higher developments in 1789–91 that principle endowed her with a distinct and vivid consciousness, so that what had been a set of limbs, worked in the main by a master, became a body-politic—nay, more, a soul-politic that defied division. In this new and intense life she exerted a singular fascination on all peoples. Thinkers felt her magnetic potency. Goethe, unresponsive to German politics, bowed before the manifestation of her uncanny strength at Valmy. Schiller and Fichte hailed her as the source of light and warmth to a dead world. Wordsworth and Coleridge first felt the full thrill of poetic ecstasy as they gazed on her civic raptures, and foretold defeat to all who withstood her new-found might. That was Nationality in its purest form. It corresponds to the time in life when the youth *finds himself*.

But, as often happens in human affairs, this strength ran riot. Self-realization begot self-confidence, and that in its turn contempt for those who were still inert. Hence the crusade of 1792 for the liberation of unfree peoples degenerated into wars of aggression. As Wordsworth phrased it:—

> "But now, become oppressors in their turn,
>   Frenchmen had changed a war of self-defence
>   For one of conquest, losing sight of all
>   Which they had struggled for. . . .
>   . . . I read her doom,
>   With anger vexed, with disappointment sore." [1]

This sudden degeneration of French Nationality reminds us that there is a baser side to the instinct. In this respect it does not aim at the union of all who desire to share in the common life, but seeks to compel aliens to come in. It uses force, not attraction. Its outcome is tyranny, not liberty; a military Empire, not a free Federation.

Not only events in France in 1792–1815, but also the

[1] Wordsworth, *Prelude*, Bk. XI.

Continental movements of 1848–9 reveal the ease with which Nationalism is perverted and becomes an enemy to freedom. When the peoples of Italy, France, Germany, and Austria-Hungary rose to demand constitutional rule and a more natural political grouping, Democracy and Nationality seemed for a time to have achieved a complete triumph. But the two principles soon clashed, especially among the Germans and Magyars. In Hungary, the Magyars won their freedom from the House of Hapsburg, but soon showed their unfitness for the boon. No sooner did they gain constitutional rights than they used them to force the Magyar language on their Slav fellow-subjects—an act of intolerance fatal to Hungary in 1849, as similar acts have been in the recent past.[1] At other points, too, the Nationalists of 1849 strained their case to breaking point, with the result that in Central Europe and to a less extent in Italy Democracy and Nationality parted company, to their mutual detriment.

The upshot of it all was that the programme of Mazzini failed in the sphere of practice; and the peoples, unable to achieve self-expression by their unaided exertions, fell back on the methods of diplomacy and force exemplified in the careers of Cavour and Bismarck, and championed by the Houses of Savoy and Hohenzollern. In that statement much lies enfolded; for it implies that they entered upon paths parallel to those which led Revolutionary France towards Militarism.

True: the successes won by Cavour and Bismarck were phenomenal. The Italian and German movements rushed to victory in the eleven years 1859–70; but I believe that all intelligent Germans now regret the suddenness and the brilliance of that triumph of military force. Better that

---

[1] Bluntschli (*Theory of the State*, Bk. II, ch. 3) says that a State cannot deny a Nationality the use of its language and literature, though it may use the predominant language for convenience.

Germany and Italy had struggled on some decades longer, and won their national unity by less forceful means and at the cost of fewer national antipathies.

Let us retrace our steps in order to observe the parallel courses of Militarism in Republican France and Bismarckian Prussia. As we saw in Lecture II, France adopted the principle of civic service for her newly enfranchised sons in 1789; and Lafayette, shortly after the capture of the Bastille, when founding the new National Guard, pronounced that force "an institution at once civic and military, which must prevail over the old tactics of Europe, and which will reduce arbitrary Governments to the alternative of being beaten if they do not imitate it, or overthrown [by their subjects] if they dare to imitate it." [1] This remarkable prophecy did not come true until the national danger became acute; but then, in the spring of 1793, the organization of the National Guards was greatly extended, so much so as to cause the first outbreaks in recalcitrant La Vendée. After the individualist Girondins were overthrown on June 2, thoroughgoing Jacobins leaped to power, and they proceeded to enforce the principle of national service. With Robespierre supreme in the Committee of Public Safety and Carnot as its military organizer, conscription became the groundwork of the national defence. In a great speech at the Jacobins' Club on August 11 Robespierre thus set forth the gravity of the military crisis: " . . . The remedy is in you yourselves. . . . If the whole people does not derive fresh courage from our reverses; if one single citizen fails to rush forward to devote himself to the salvation of the country by beating back its oppressors, it is all up with Liberty: she will not survive our courage." Thereafter a Report was presented to the National Convention urging drastic measures, because "half measures are always fatal in extreme peril. The whole nation is easier to move than a

[1] Lafayette, *Méms.*, II, 267.

part of the nation. . . . Let there be no exceptions save those which are necessary for the sowing and harvesting of the crops." Barère then declared that the whole nation ought to rise in defence of freedom and constitution and to drive out the foreign despots and their satellites. On August 23 the National Convention placed all males of military age permanently at the service of the armies. The decree ran thus: "The young men shall go to fight; married men shall forge weapons and transport supplies; the women shall make tents and uniforms or serve in the hospitals; the children shall make lint; the old men shall be carried to the public squares to excite the courage of soldiers, hatred of kings, and enthusiasm for the unity of the Republic." [1] That is how France interpreted the new device on its flags: "The French nation risen against tyrants."

It has been asserted that the decree of 1798 is the first law of conscription. True, it carried out more methodically the system imposed in August, 1793. But the later decree was merely the extension of the earlier decree, which gave France those massive arrays so fatal to the thin lines of Coburg and the Duke of York. The momentum of the new national forces carried them into Holland, the Rhineland, and the Genoese Riviera in the campaigns of 1794–5, thus inaugurating the period of conquest, which was prolonged by the genius and ambition of Napoleon.

These facts should be noted carefully; for they dispose of the assertions often made, that conscription was a device of the monarchs for the enslavement of their peoples. Far from that, conscription was a device of the most democratic government in the world for the expulsion of the armies of the monarchs. None of them dared to copy the democratic principle of national service, until Frederick William III of Prussia doubtfully adopted it as a desperate expedient for

[1] *Hist. parlementaire*, XXVIII, 455–469.

saving that humiliated State from utter ruin; and the Prussian
army, when nationalized, played a very important part in the
overthrow of Napoleon. I believe that there is a vague
notion that conscription originated with him. He merely
systematized its application. The responsibility for the
introduction of the system lies with the French Republicans
of 1793 and 1798. It was therefore a result of the national
and democratic sentiment which swept through France at the
time of her great Revolution. The statement that Militarism
is the outcome of a deep-laid plot of rulers to enslave their
peoples is so far wrong, that, after the Restoration of the
French Bourbons in 1814–5, the national army was con-
siderably reduced; and the same thing happened among
other peoples. Autocrats do not like universal service; for
they cannot trust it. Thus ended Militarism in its first
phase.

The second, or Prussian, phase began in 1860, when, for
purposes of defence, after the humiliations of the previous
years, the Regent (soon King), William I of Prussia, introduced the first of his famous Army Bills. They were fiercely
opposed by the Prussian Parliament in the belief that he
would make the army the tool of absolutism. But his aim was
patriotic, not despotic. After the overthrow of Denmark and
Austria by means of that army, Prussian Liberals withdrew
their opposition and condoned all the illegal proceedings of
years 1860–6. Why? Because, however high-handed, the
the Bismarckian policy had enabled them to win Schleswig-
Holstein from the Danes and to weld the North German
States on the firm basis of the Prussian monarchy. Their
constitutional scruples vanished when it appeared that the
policy of "blood and iron" had prevailed over two neighboring States, and had nearly solved the problem of German
unity. The Prussian deputies now saw that the King's aim
had been national. The triumph of 1870 clinched the success

of Prussia; and the German Empire of 1871, though federal in form, was, in effect, an enlargement of Prussia. In March, 1849, King Frederick William IV had solemnly promised that Prussia should merge herself in Germany. In 1871 Germany merged herself in Prussia.

The brilliance of these military triumphs led neighboring peoples to copy the Prussian army; and once again Europe became an armed camp. The results are well known. Just as Napoleon diverted to purposes of conquest a citizen-army which at first was solely defensive, so Kaiser Wilhelm II has misused the enormous resources of men, arms, and money which his grandfather is believed to have amassed primarily for the sake of defence. Worst of all, the national army which enabled Prussia in 1866-70 to effect the unity of Germany, has been prostituted to colossal schemes of aggrand-izement at the expense of weaker neighbors. The conduct of Wilhelm II in this century therefore resembles that of Napoleon a century ago. But in one respect the Hohen-zollern has less excuse than the Corsican. In the years 1805-15 national sentiment was far less developed than it is to-day. A century of effort has strengthened the individuality of all the peoples, so that their merging in any one State or Union, which was possible under Napoleon, is unthinkable under Wilhelm. Prussia now offers her victims no high ideal of citizenship, only the prospect of unlimited drilling with a view to the subjection of other peoples; no inspiring traditions such as glorified the French Empire—little else than records of astute opportunism, sudden attack, and now, as in 1871, brutality in the hour of real or fancied triumph. Such is the history of fifty-five years of Prussian Militarism. Under Napoleon (at any rate up to Friedland, 1807) the French polity had not so far belied its democratic origin as to be a tool of despotism and ambition. The men who carried Napoleon's eagles to Vienna, Rome, and Warsaw believed that they were furthering the cause of liberty. Do the German troops in Belgium, Poland, and Serbia believe that? Will a foreign poet and a foreign composer ever sound forth the heroism and chivalry of *zwei Grenadieren*, as Heine and Schumann immortalized those of Napoleon?

LECTURE IX

NATIONALISM SINCE 1885

"Weak and incapable nations must look on while foreign nationalities gain in number and importance within the borders of their State."—PRINCE VON BÜLOW, *Imperial Germany*, p. 240.

THE previous studies have illustrated the excellences and defects of the national movements up to the year 1885. The instinct of Nationality has endowed the European peoples and Japan (perhaps soon we shall add China) with a vitality and force which resembles, say, the incoming of steam-power into industry. What previously had been minutely subdivided and inert became united, vigorous, aggressive. Contrast the ridiculous Germany at which Heine mocked, the torpid Italy which Mazzini awakened, with the great and powerful nations of to-day. The changes wrought by the national wars of the years 1859–70 are among the most important of all time; for they altered not only the polity but the national character in France, Germany, and Italy.[1] Further, the Balkan peoples were nerved to struggle for their rights, and in 1876–8 and 1885 they largely succeeded in shaking off the Turkish yoke. In the autumn of 1885 the union of the two Bulgarias almost completed the aspira-

---

[1] In a Paris paper early in February, 1871, was an article by "Ferragus" which began: "Bismarck has probably done better service to France than to Germany. He has worked for a false unity in his country, but very effectually for a regeneration of ours. He has freed us from the Empire. He has restored to us our energy, our hatred for the foreigner, our love for our country, our contempt for life, our readiness for self-sacrifice, in short all the virtues which Napoleon III had killed in us."

tions of that people; and (as we saw in Lecture VI) it enabled them to escape from Russian tutelage and to proceed with internal developments of great promise. On the other hand British policy, which under Lord Beaconsfield had thwarted the national efforts of the Balkan peoples, now, under Lord Salisbury, resumed its traditional rôle of protector of the small nationalities. Thus, up to the month of September, 1885, Nationalism won portentous triumphs. True, in 1866 Prussia overstepped her fair limits by annexing the Danes of North Schleswig, and in 1871 by wrenching Alsace-Lorraine from France. Still, the balance was decidedly favorable for the national principle.

We now approach events of a different order. I propose to review them here as impartially as possible, and in the main to leave you to draw your own conclusions.

On November 14, 1885, King Milan of Serbia suddenly declared war against Bulgaria on a frivolous pretext, his real reason being jealousy of the increase of her power consequent on the recent union. The Serbs entered Bulgaria, and were advancing towards Sofia, when the Bulgars, speedily rallying, soundly beat them at Slivnitza, and chased them back into their own territory. Near Pirot the victors were bidden to halt. The Austrian general, Khevenhüller, declared in imperious terms that any further advance would oblige the Dual-Monarchy to send in its white-coats. The Bulgars thereafter retired, and patched up matters with Serbia; but the incident rankled in the breasts of both peoples and excited racial jealousies dating back five centuries to the time of Serbia's glory under the sway of King Dushan.

The collision has a double significance. Only seven years after deliverance from their bondage to the Turk two Christian peoples flew at one another's throats and thereby provoked hatreds whose ghastly sequel has recently appalled

the world. Secondly, the intervention of Austria on behalf
of her *protégé*, King Milan, gave color to the story that she
had incited him to that fratricidal attack in order to weaken
the Balkan peoples and thus prepare the way for her advance
southwards to Salonica. As she had bargained with the Tsar
in 1876 with a view to the acquisition of that long-coveted
port,[1] she probably had a hand in Milan's enterprise. Thereafter both he and his son, Alexander (the latter reigned at
Belgrade from 1889 to 1903) were notoriously under Hapsburg patronage, which often screened them from the resentment of the Serb people. The murder of Alexander and the
accession of Peter (of the Karageorge family) inaugurated
a national policy, which increasingly incurred the displeasure
of the Hapsburgs. But, despite the long tutelage of Serbia
by them, and that of Bulgaria by the Tsar Alexander III;
even despite the cruelties of the Sultan Abdul Hamid II
against both the Serbs and Bulgars in Macedonia, these races
could not lay aside their mutual hatreds. Consequently,
the ideal of a Balkan Federation remained a dream; and
disgust at the narrow and vindictive Nationalism of the
Balkan peoples probably figured among the motives which
led the new Tsar, Nicholas II (1894–1917), to turn away from
their exasperating feuds towards the golden visions opening
out in the Far East. Whatever his reasons, he certainly took
less interest than his father in Balkan affairs.

   In 1897 the Greeks struggled unsuccessfully to extend
their too narrow bounds in Thessaly. They met with no
support whatever from Serbs and Bulgars, and succumbed
to an unexpectedly sharp counter-stroke from Turks and
Albanians. In the same year ruthless massacres of Macedonians and Armenians by order of Abdul Hamid mani-
fested his resolve to effect a Moslem revival by the traditional Turkish method; and the sight of this energy produced

   [1] Debidour, *Hist. diplomatique de l'Europe*, II, 515.

no small impression at Berlin. In face of these glaring violations of the articles of the Treaty of 1878, guaranteeing good government to the Christian subjects of the Sultan, Great Britain, France, and Italy displayed an apathy highly discreditable to their rulers. Their inaction in a matter closely concerning their honor, the orientation of Russian policy, and the warlike prowess of Abdul Hamid served to strengthen a Panislam movement, which soon received a public benediction from Kaiser Wilhelm II. During his Eastern tour in 1898 (that is, two years after the adoption of *Weltpolitik*) he announced his resolve to befriend the Sultan and the 300,000,000 Moslems—a declaration destined to strengthen Mohammedan fanaticism and to cause further massacres of the Christians of the Ottoman Empire. Further troubles having ensued, especially in that seething cauldron of races, Macedonia, the Emperors of Russia and Austria drew up at Mürzsteg in 1903 a programme of reforms for an improved administration of that province.[1] The "Mürzsteg Programme" completed and strengthened one that the two Sovereigns had framed in 1897, the other Powers on both occasions agreeing to delegate special functions to those previously rival Empires. Both efforts to put down anarchy in Macedonia failed, either from lack of energy in the efforts, or because the racial feuds were insoluble. Accordingly, the Great Powers once more took up the duties imposed on them by the Treaty of Berlin, and in April, 1907, sought to cure the maladministration of Macedonia. This attempt came too late; for the situation had recently changed in

[1] Very many Macedonians have no definite racial affinity, which enables rival claimants to number the Greeks either 600,000 or 200,000; the Bulgars, 2,000,000, 1,500,000, or 60,000; the Serbs 2,050,000 or nil; the Wallachs 100,000 or 75,000; the Turks 600,000 or 230,000. See J. Cvijic, *Remarques sur l'Ethnographie de la Macédoine;* Ichircoff, *Etude ethnographique sur les Slaves de Macédoine* (Paris, 1908).

favor of the Central Empires. Russia was badly beaten by Japan in 1904-5, whereupon the Berlin Government dictated terms to France in the Moroccan affair of 1905-6; and, with the accession of Aehrenthal to office, in 1906, Austria entered upon a vigorous foreign policy. The results were seen in an increase of Teutonic energy in all quarters, while the Slav cause, which Russia had neglected since 1897, underwent a notable decline, the prestige of Austria and Turkey proportionately rising.

These facts explain the daring stroke of Austria in annexing Bosnia outright; while at the same time her *protégé*, Prince Ferdinand of Bulgaria, proclaimed himself Tsar of the Bulgarians (October, 1908). Coming soon after the Young Turk Revolution at Constantinople, these events foreshadowed a future in which Austria, Bulgaria, and a renovated Turkey would share the Peninsula about equally between them. Germany threw her weight into the scale in favor of Austria; and a threat from Kaiser Wilhelm to Russia in the spring of 1909 caused the latter to accept the Hapsburgs' *fait accompli* in Bosnia. Thenceforth the future of the Balkans lay with the Central Empires and with their *protégés*, Bulgaria and Roumania.

To the confusion caused by threats from without were added the miseries due to ever-increasing racial feuds and mad misgovernment. The Young Turks, far from carrying out their much-vaunted programme of reforms, soon exasperated their subjects by an "Ottomanizing" policy of the most pedantic and irritating kind. Consequently, the Greek, Serb, and Bulgar elements in Macedonia despaired of obtaining redress except by force, and what the Turkish vampires spared the armed bands of these rival races swept off. The beginning of the end came for Ottoman rule when the usually faithful Albanians rose in revolt against stupid interferences with their customs and language. Consequently, the Eastern Question in 1909–12 entered upon its last and most terrible phase.

While Nationalism in the Balkans made more and more for strife, the same instinct waxed powerful and aggressive in Central Europe. The interaction of these cyclonic systems has finally produced the present appalling tempest. In order to understand that interaction and the tremendous forces which it set in motion, we must retrace our steps and note the rise of Chauvinism in Germany and the outlet which it sought to acquire towards the East.

As we have already seen, Kaiser Wilhelm II has modelled his policy largely on that of Frederick the Great. Now, during that reign, as also subsequently, Prussia often made use of the Turks to annoy and weaken either Russia or Austria, whenever those realms were at feud with her. Another fact is equally significant. The rival Houses of Hapsburg and Hohenzollern have rarely continued long in close union except for purposes of aggression against their neighbors. Cases in point are their agreements to effect the Partitions of Poland (1772, 1793, 1795, though in 1793 Austria complained of being left in the lurch) and those of 1792 and 1815 for the annexation of large portions of France. In 1827–30 they united in order to thwart the emancipation of Greece, then championed by Russia, France, and England, the general aim of the Germanic Powers being to uphold Turkish authority and stay the growth of the Christian peoples of the Balkans.[1] But that negative and cramping policy has of late given way to one that has sought to range Turkey, if possible along with Roumania and Bulgaria, on the side of the Central Empires. Serb nationalists, inspired by jealousy of Bulgaria and the

---

[1] See, too, Debidour, *Hist. diplomatique de l'Europe*, II, 181–3, for Austria's opposition to the formation of the Principality of Roumania in 1858, which was helped on by Russia and Napoleon III, "the friend of nationalities."

hope of detaching their kith and kin, the Croats and Slovenes, from Austria, firmly opposed all attempts at bullying or bargaining from Vienna. But the stolid Tartar strain in the Bulgars' nature afforded some hope of rallying them, under their Coburg prince, to the side of their Moslem oppressors and against their Russian liberators. This done, Serbia alone barred the way to the formation of a Teutonic-Magyar-Turanian League, extending from the North Sea to the Persian Gulf. For such a purpose Hohenzollern and Hapsburg might well clasp hands and consort with the butchers of the Balkan Christians. That this Eastern expansion would crush Balkan Nationalism was nothing to the leaders of thought and action in the Central Empires; for their conception of things had wholly changed since the time when Bismarck and Deàk achieved the triumph of that principle for the German and the Magyar.

Let us, then, review the events which transformed Bismarck's Austro-German alliance of 1879 (an essentially defensive compact) into an aggressive league aiming at the domination of the land hemisphere. The determining event was the accession of Kaiser Wilhelm II to the German throne in 1888. Inheriting a powerful and prosperous domain, protected by an invincible army and unassailable alliances, he nevertheless declared in his first proclamation that he would ever be responsible for the glory and honor of his army. To this was added keen solicitude for naval and colonial expansion, as appeared in his very profitable bargain with Lord Salisbury in 1890 for the cession of some untenable claims over Zanzibar against the acquisition of that valuable naval base, Heligoland. But the fact that he bargained anything away in East Africa angered the more eager of the German patriots, who sought to prevent a recurrence of such a humiliation by founding a kind of watchdog Society in 1891, which, three years later, became the Pangerman League. Claiming that the German Empire must become a World-Empire, it set forth the following ideal: "Above the interests of the State should be those of the Nation. Even more sacred than love of the Fatherland should be love of the Motherland." It soon appeared that the nation was the totality of all German-speaking peoples, and the Motherland was the area (geographically vague but mentally stimulating) which would bring all these peoples into the Teutonic fellowship. The Germans of Austria, Switzerland, and the Baltic provinces of Russia (though the last were but a small minority among the Letts and Esthonians) were all to be swept into the Motherland's arms, which would finally close around Dutch, Flemings, and Scandinavians. The day of little States and little peoples was over; for they lived a narrow existence, oppressed by fear of vigorous neighbors. Let them, therefore, merge their miserable lives in that of the Teutonic Superman. Such was the Pangerman propaganda, directed by a friend of the Kaiser, Dr. Hasse. It soon gained an immense vogue; and around the League clustered several organizations, chief among them the Navy League.

The generation which grew up during the years of König-grätz and Sedan (William II's generation) was in the mood to regard even those triumphs as precursors to others of world-wide import. Merely by skilful carpet-bagging and diplomatic hustling, Bismarck and agents like Peters, Nachtigall, and Lüdertiz had secured a considerable colonial Empire; and if that were gained by craft, what might not be the outcome of a well-prepared effort of the whole German nation? After the surrender of Paris in January, 1871, Bismarck called his people "the male principle, the fructifying principle" of Europe; while the Celts and Slavs represented the female sex. As for the English, they were contemptible hucksters, envious of the brave Germans but afraid to fight them.[1] Such was the doctrine taught to young Germany in and after 1871. To it Treitschke merely added an academic veneer. Viewing history from the standpoint of a patriotic pamphleteer, he excited the youth of Germany by sentences such as these: "To tell the truth, the Slav seems to us a born slave";[2] or again: "What nation will impose its will on the other enfeebled and decadent peoples? Will it not be Germany's mission to ensure the peace of the world? Russia, that immense Colossus with feet of clay, will be absorbed in its domestic and economic difficulties. England, stronger in appearance than in reality, will doubtless see her colonies break loose and exhaust themselves in fruitless struggles. France, given over to internal dissensions and the strife of parties, will sink into hopeless decadence. As to Italy, she will have her work cut out to ensure a crust to her children. The future belongs to Germany, to which Austria will attach herself if she wishes to survive." With a few honorable exceptions the teachers at the German Universities adopted this tone, and thus nursed the feeling of national pride which the parade ground brought to lush maturity.

Along with this, however, there grew up a passion to excel, to push through every task to thorough completion. An English correspondent long in Germany has described it by their word *Drang*—driving force, or the resolve to make your will prevail.[3] It is a formidable force in all departments of life, and contrasts sharply with the easy good nature and weak tolerance of bad work far too prevalent among us. In this respect we need to copy the Germans and regain that passion for thoroughness which used to be

---

[1] *Bismarck: some secret Pages of his History*, I, 500, 526; *Bismarck in the Franco-German War*, I, 277, II, 8, 19, 333, 345 (note).

[2] Treitschke, *Germany, France, Russia, and Islam* (Eng. edit.), p. 17.

[3] C. Tower, *Changing Germany*, p. 255.

ours, but which has vanished of late under the influence of
pleasure, sport, or the worship of the eight-hours' day. It
is significant that the German phrase *Alles in Ordnung*,
which corresponds to our "All right," conveys a guarantee
that all is right. Whereas our phrase "All right" has come
to mean: "Now, don't bother: I've done all I mean to
do." This is the spirit which we must drive from our Universities and schools, our workshops and public offices. We
need a new sense of the dignity of work such as Thomas
Carlyle hammered into his generation—a healthy public
opinion which will be stronger than official etiquette, stronger
than red tape, stronger even than Trade Union regulations.
In this respect Germany has much to teach us regarding
her matchless power of organization; and at bottom that
means power of hard work and clear thinking. In the fierce
competition of the modern world (a competition which will be
fiercer than ever after the war) no nation is sure of holding
its own unless it puts forth its utmost powers, directs them
wisely, and minimizes the friction between Capital and
Labor.

To return to Germany: the intense devotion of her people,
fostered in the schools and Universities, has permeated all
parts of the national life; and it must be remembered that
that feeling, with its counterpart, contempt for other peoples,
is based on a not unnatural belief in the primacy of Germans
in all important spheres. Thus a new tone has permeated
the German people during the reign of Wilhelm II. It has
also profoundly affected their settlers in other lands, who,
under the influence of patriotic clubs, have tended to form
garrisons for the Empire, ready, when called upon, to take
action against the communities out of which they have
made their money. No harm would have resulted from
this fanatical Teutonism if the Kaiser and his paladins had
been wise and prudent. But startling results followed when

he, they and the leading professors and journalists sought to outcrow each other in praise of Germania. Sheer political vertigo was the outcome, especially since 1896, when Wilhelm proclaimed *Welpolitik* as the goal of her efforts. The Pangerman League first enunciated the programme in 1894. Not to be outdone, the Kaiser adopted it at the twenty-fifth anniversary of the proclamation of the Empire (January 21, 1896).

In other matters the League has pushed him on. In 1895 it urged the acquisition of a good naval base in China; the mailed fist in 1897 descended upon Kiao-Chao, after the opportune murder of two German missionaries. In 1896 the League earmarked Asia Minor as a fit sphere for economic penetration by the Germans. Again after an interval of two years, the Kaiser proceeded to Constantinople and Damascus, making at the tomb of Saladin his promise ever to champion the Moslem-World. In 1896–7 the Pangerman and Navy Leagues began a systematic agitation in favor of a great navy. The Kaiser responded by appointing Admiral von Tirpitz to the Admiralty, and an expansionist, Count (now Prince) von Bülow, to the Foreign Office; while the Navy Bill of 1898 ushered in the long series of measures for the systematic and sustained increase of the German marine. Certain acts of the Kaiser, such as his proclamation as to *Weltpolitik*, bear the impress of his personality, which loves to seize a great occasion for the utterance of a sonorous and telling phrase. But in the main it seems that he has been pushed on by eager and ambitious patriots, who, after gaining the ear of a morbidly sensitive public, have reproached him for timidity whenever he has sought to steady the pace.

It is worthy of note that he has given them their head on occasions when he deemed Germany to be well prepared for war. Such occasions were the years succeeding the opening of the Kiel Canal in 1895; the completion of the first instalment of the new navy in 1905 (which coincided with Russia's defeats in the Far East); the opportunity which offered for supporting Austria's forward move of October, 1908, in the Near East; and the completion of the enlarged Kiel Canal in June, 1914 (which coincided with singular difficulties for the Entente Powers and a unique state of military preparation in Germany). On other occasions he has often held in the Pangermans despite their champing the bit and pawing the air. But again, as if to relieve his pent-up feelings, he has uttered words that struck like a spur: "Our future lies on the water"—"The trident must pass into our hands"—"We are the salt of the earth"—"The German nation alone has been called upon to defend, cultivate, and develop great ideas"—"Our German nation shall be the rock of granite on which the Almighty will finish his work of civilizing the world. Then shall be fulfilled the words of the poet: 'German character shall save the world.'" The ruler who uttered these words, and tried to live up to them, must bear a heavy share of responsibility for the growth of an overweening Chauvinism. The collective impulse, which up to 1870 had been a healthy endeavor to achieve national union, has under Kaiser Wilhelm II been degraded into an aggressive Nationalism utterly callous of the claims of other peoples.

Rash in word but prudent in deed, Wilhelm kept a tight curb on his high-spirited charger until a clear field was before him; and in this respect he may count as the new Machiavel. During the Boer War of 1899–1902 he turned the furiously Anglophobe passions of his subjects into a practical channel by carrying through an immense naval programme; and in the spring of 1905, when Russia's military power tottered under the blows of Japan, he embarked on the Moroccan policy which the Leagues had pressed on him long before.

Meanwhile his Chancellor, Bülow, had secured the passing
of the Tariff Laws of 1902 for the protection of agriculture
so that the Germany of the future might not depend too
largely on foreign foodstuffs. A further aim of the Kaiser
and Chancellor was to stimulate tillage of the soil so as to
maintain a healthy balance between industry and agriculture, as was summed up in the phrase, "Agriculture must
provide soldiers and industry pay for them." [1]

Thus was built up a polity no less prosperous in peace
than well prepared for war; and the outcome of this material
preparedness and national confidence was seen in the rebuffs
dealt to France in the Moroccan affair of 1905–6. Apprehension of Germany had prompted the Anglo-French Entente of 1904, and in 1907 came that between England and
Russia, which was clinched by the recent declarations of
Germany at the Hague Conference, that she would neither
lessen her armaments nor submit disputes to arbitration.
The Ententes, though merely conditional agreements far
removed from definite alliances, ought to have warned the
German people of the need of lowering its tone. In normal
conditions a nation would regard the alienation of an old
friend, like Russia, and her drawing towards other States
for protection, as a sign that its conduct had been unduly
provocative, and that bluster must give way to conciliation.
But this is not the way of champions of *Drang*. Their aim
being to carry matters with a high hand, they interpret all
signs of distrust as a challenge to their honor. Newly awakened Nationalism (and that of Germany dates from 1870)
has always displayed the morbid sensitiveness of youth, and
has given out that the Entente is contriving a villainous plot
to "encircle" Germany and Austria with a view to bringing about their isolation and destruction.

Let us examine this charge in the light of facts. They are

[1] Bülow, *Imperial Germany*, pp. 209–11.

as follows: The Central Empires had a close alliance with Italy and a personal compact with the King of Roumania, a member of the Swabian branch of the House of Hohenzollern. A German prince reigned over Bulgaria, the Kaiser's sister had married the Crown Prince of Greece, and the Sultan of Turkey was notoriously a satrap of Berlin. Consequently, the "encircling" of a block of territory, which extended from the North Sea to the Tyrrhene and Ægean, could scarcely be taken seriously by those who knew the facts of the case. But by dint of much noise and skilful suppression of facts, the Germans, and not a few Englishmen, were led to regard the Central Empires, etc., as pinched in by wily and aggressive foes under the direction of the arch-plotter, King Edward VII. The theory of "encircling" proved to be especially serviceable in dulling the opposition of German Socialists to the successive Army and Navy Bills. Unacquainted with military history, they failed to realize the enormous advantage of the central position in warfare; and the authorities, who every year increased that advantage by constructing strategic railways to the western and eastern frontiers, ceased not to alarm their subjects as to the terrible might of the Eastern Colossus, the quenchless thirst of Frenchmen for a war of revenge, and the malignant jealousy of England.

That the German Government was not actuated by fear of Russia or France is obvious from its policy. At the Hague Conference of 1907, as we have seen, it rejected all proposals for arbitration and limitation of armaments; at the close of 1908 the Reichstag passed Bills for the Germanizing of Alsace-Lorrainers, the Poles of Posen, and the Danes of North Schleswig. At the same time Germany supported her ally, Austria, in her annexation of Bosnia; and in March, 1909, a threatening note from Berlin to Petrograd led the Tsar to withdraw his opposition to that step. Further, the vigorous efforts of Teutonic diplomacy to recover the ground at first lost at Constantinople in the Young Turk Revolution of 1908 were completely successful. This forceful policy upheld the arms of Austria-Hungary, browbeat Russia, and encouraged the Young Turks to proceed with the "Ottomanizing" of their Christian subjects.[1]

In no quarter did the Teutonic idea work more effectively than in Austria-Hungary. In its early stages the Pangerman movement seemed to threaten the disruption of the Dual Monarchy, whose Germanic subjects, hard pressed by Slavs and Magyars, seemed likely to break away from the crumbling heritage of the Hapsburgs and form a southern annexe of the Hohenzollern Empire. But, however much the Pangermans played with the notion, the statesmen of Berlin finally discouraged it as tending to form a diffuse realm in which Prussian influence would be lost.[2] They deemed it better to favor the German elements in Austria and support that Empire in the difficult enterprise of dominating the Balkans. In 1906 the Archduke Ferdinand and the new Foreign Minister, Aehrenthal, inaugurated a spirited foreign policy which succeeded in quieting, or crushing, racial strifes within the Empire. The revival of the prestige of the Dual Monarchy was assisted by the passionate Nationalism of the Magyars, which at times amounted almost to frenzy. Excited by the celebrations of the thousandth anniversary of their organized national life in 1896, Hungarian patriots had resolved to ride roughshod over their Slavonic and Roumanian subjects; and their exuberant patriotism reduced parliamentary elections and procedure

[1] *Nationalism and War in the Near East,* by "Diplomatist," chs. III, IV.

[2] G. Weil, *Le Pangermanisme en Autriche,* chs. 7, 8. But the revelations of Mr. Wickham Steed (*Nineteenth Century,* Feb., 1916) as to the alleged bargain between Kaiser Wilhelm and the Archduke Franz Ferdinand in June, 1914, seem to show that the former may then have revived the older Pangerman scheme.

to the level of a farce; while their sense of justice received
startling illustration in incidents such as that of the Agram
trial.[1] Nevertheless this crude Nationalism succeeded for
the time; and, joining hands with the boisterous anti-Semites
of Vienna and the expansionists of Berlin, it prepared to
stride southwards to conquest over the hated Serbs.

Austro-Hungarian Chauvinism secured its first triumph
in the annexation of Bosnia and Herzegovina in October,
1908. The significance of this event was doubled by its coin-
cidence with the assumption of the title "Tsar of the Bulgarians" by Prince Ferdinand of Bulgaria immediately after
a visit to the Hapsburg Court. Half Austrian by upbringing,
and largely Magyar by sympathy and territorial connections,
that wily schemer by his title now laid claim to lordship
over the large Bulgar population of Macedonia; and Austria's
longings for Salonica being notorious, it was clear that the
Dual Monarchy and her satrap were contemplating an eventual partition of that troublous province. In view of the
decline of Russia's prestige in the Near East since her disastrous adventures in the Far East, the Central Empires
and their pro-consuls at Sofia and Bukarest had in their
hands the future of the Balkan Peninsula.

These brilliant successes, I repeat, rehabilitated the prestige of Austria, stilled her racial disputes, and reduced the
Serbs and their Croat cousins to despair. The details of the
compromise framed by the Pangermans and the Dual Monarchy are, of course, not known; but the success of Austria's
forward and Teutonic policy, as contrasted with the barren
parliamentary and racial strifes of the earlier period, opened
up a new and promising future, in which it seemed that
Austria-Hungary would be predominantly German-Magyar
and would control the Balkans, thus forming an essential

[1] See Dr. Seton-Watson's works, *Corruption and Reform in Hungary,
Racial Problems in Hungary,* etc.

link in the future Zollverein stretching from the North Sea
to the Bosphorus, the Persian Gulf, and the Red Sea. As
this scheme developed, it naturally aroused alarm in Russia
and among the Mediterranean Powers. The Italians began
to sheer off from the Triple Alliance as its Oriental ambitions
developed; and fear of Austro-German aggressions grouped
Great Britain, France, and Russia more closely together.
The Franco-German agreement of 1909 respecting Morocco
did not, and could not, solve that question; while the Russo-
German compact arrived at late in 1910 failed to compose
their rivalries in the Near East.

   This brief survey will suffice to explain not only the political
tension prevalent throughout Europe but also the growth
of a neurotic Nationalism in Germany. Not satisfied with
her supremacy in Europe, she prepared to achieve world-
dominance; and the military weakness of Russia, together
with the absorption of France and England in parliamentary
disputes, furthered her schemes. The Western Powers
sought to solve social questions by concessions and bargains;
Germany prepared to solve them by distracting the attention
of the masses to national issues. Prince Bülow has frankly
avowed that intention. He states that the successive Army
and Navy Bills were designed to help on Germany's world-
policy, and, in order to secure a majority in the Reichstag,
the middle classes and as many as possible of the working
classes had to be won over. He admits that, notwithstanding
all the efforts put forth against the Social Democrats, their
votes at the polls steadily mounted, though the number of
seats gained curiously varied.

Votes polled.	Seats gained.
1898...2,107,000	56
1903...3,011,000	81
1907...3,539,000	43
1912...4,250,000	110

Their losses of seats in 1907 were due to speeches, explanations, and "the direction of the electoral compaign." [1] As to the Socialist gains of 1912, Bülow says nothing, because they were due to the spirited protests of that party against *Weltpolitik*. On the general question of combating the Socialists, he says: "We must accustom them to the idea of the State. . . . The idea of the nation must again and again be emphasized by dealing with national problems, so that this idea may continue to move, unite, and separate the parties. Nothing has a more discouraging, paralyzing, and depressing effect on a clever, enterprising, and highly developed nation such as the Germans than a monotonous, dull policy, which, for fear of an ensuing fight, avoids rousing passions by strong action." Bülow also advised the Government to fight Social Democracy by "a great and comprehensive national policy." By this he declares that he meant the Germanizing of all the races within the Empire, especially the Poles, whose political incompetence had subjected them to the superior organization of Prussia. But he deprecated the conquest of neighboring territories. [2]

Such a limitation of Germany's expansive power displeased German Chauvinists, who exercised greater pressure on Bülow's successor, Bethmann-Hollweg (1909–   ). The Foreign Assistant Secretary, Kiderlen-Waechter, favored the Agadir *coup* of July, 1911, which is known to have been contrived by the Navy and other patriotic Leagues. First, they pointed out in the Press the urgent need of German expansion in Morocco; and then the two Ministers declared that they must try to keep pace with public opinion. Thus the mutually exciting influences of the Leagues and the Administration worked up a furious national feeling which formed the

[1] Bülow, *Imperial Germany*, pp. 158–168. The total number of deputies is 397.

[2] *Ibid.*, pp. 157–204, 239–245.

chief danger of the situation. The dispute at Agadir in itself was trivial, as was afterwards admitted by German patriots. But their masterful tone nearly brought about a general war. Probably this was their aim; for great was their wrath when the Kaiser and his Ministry finally patched up the Morocco dispute by the compact of November 4, 1911, with France, gaining about 100,000 square miles of French Congoland at the price of their acquiescence in French supremacy in Morocco. The rage of German Chauvinists against the Kaiser for this profitable though inglorious bargain burst out in downright insults, *Die Post* calling him *ce poltron misérable*.[1]

In a short time the Germans saw that they had exaggerated the importance of the Moroccan affair. In 1912 that astute publicist, Maximilian Harden, said: "As for the Morocco escapade, God knows the colonial fever was there expended for nothing. It was simply an affair of prestige,—national prestige, personal prestige. Germany had no real interests in Morocco." The Pangerman champion, Count Reventlow, also blamed that adventure as ill-judged because it offended both England and France. Nevertheless the Pangermans stirred up indignation against that "failure" in order to effect and increase the already formidable armaments. The expenditure on the army was increased by £6,450,000, despite the incidence of a severe financial crisis in 1911. A prominent German newspaper stated that a

[1] Dr. Rohrbach (*Der deutsche Gedanke in der Welt*, p. 216) declared that Germany took the wrong turn about Morocco, which was not a vital affair; besides the Hedjaz Railway, the Kiel-North Sea Canal and the forts at Heligoland were not then in readiness. In the future, too, the stake must be a greater one than a strip of Moroccan coast. He concludes: "We are now (1912) in a position to launch out boldly." Rohrbach is a champion of the Bagdad and other Levantine schemes, which will probably prove to be the chief cause of the present war. Certainly they interested Austria and Turkey, *which Morocco never did*.

great war would be "perhaps delayed, but not averted, if German armaments are not of a nature to intimidate every adversary into beating a retreat." That is the essential thought at the bottom of German Nationalism of the *Sturm und Drang* type.[1]

The formation of the Balkan League and its successful attack upon Turkey in the autumn of 1912 caused great concern in Germany and Austria, where the triumph of the crescent had been taken for granted. At once the Central Empires declared the new League to be a mere tool of Russia; whereas it was certainly the outcome of the grinding pressure of the Young Turks on all their Christian subjects. M. Sazonoff, the Russian Foreign Minister, at first discouraged the Leaguers and advised them to come to terms with Turkey.[2] As is well known, after the conclusion of a Balkan peace in London in the spring of 1913, the Christian States fell out, and, probably under the impulse of Austria, the Bulgar troops in June, 1913, perfidiously attacked the Greeks and Serbs, only to suffer condign punishment. Finally, the Treaty of Bukarest (largely decided by the two Central Empires) imposed the present unsatisfactory frontiers and left all the races of the Peninsula at feud (August, 1913). Their friction kindled the spark which set Europe in a blaze in August, 1914.[3]

---

[1] Bourdon, *The German Enigma*, pp. 158, 180, 198. Prof. Van Vollenhoven (*War Obviated by an International Police*, 1910, p. 7) calls them "force-monomaniacs." They were long laughed at in Germany, but carried the day in July, 1914.

[2] For proofs see I. E. Gueshoff, *The Balkan League* (Eng. transl.), pp. 9–45.

[3] *Ibid.*, pp. 71–94. As to Austria's responsibility for the war of 1913 (not yet fully proven) see "Balkanicus," *The Aspirations of Bulgaria* (1915), pp. 132–42. Very significant were the remarks of the Austrian *Reichspost* (the organ of the Archduke Ferdinand): "The results of the Balkan War (of 1913) have no disagreeable features for the Austro-

Here again, then, the principle of Nationality, for which
Gladstone pleaded and Stambuloff struggled, has undergone
dire degradation. Promising to sort out the Balkan peoples
according to ethnic affinities, it has of late aroused their
baser passions and lent itself to intriguers who have ruined
their people and deluged the Peninsula with blood. The
part recently played by Bulgaria completes the career of
infamy on which she entered in June, 1913. Owing all that
she is to the principle of Slav Nationality and to the powerful
aid of Russia, she has acted as Judas both to the principle
and to her champion. In order to stab Serbia in the back
she has helped her age-long oppressors, the Turks, and those
more recent and more formidable enemies of Balkan independence, the Germanic Empires.

To all who were not blinded by revenge or blinkered by
mere peasant-cunning, it ought to have been clear that the
Austro-German intrigues with the Sublime Porte for predominance in the Near East involved the suppression of
all the free races which lay in their path; that, consequently,
the subjection of Serbia in the present war would but prelude
the subjection of Bulgaria. The Teutonic-Turanian policy,
summed up in the Bagdad Railway scheme, is based on
military and trading considerations, in which Belgrade and
Sofia figure merely as stages on the route from Berlin to
Bagdad and the Persian Gulf. What would be the lot of
Turkey in case of the triumph of the new imperial commercialism is far from clear. That the lot of Bulgaria, Serbia,
and probably of Roumania and Greece, would be one of
political impotence, no student of German developments can
harbor a doubt. Such a finale to the present war would
imply the extinction of Serbia and the reversal of all that
Roumans, Greeks, Bulgars have achieved with the help of

Hungarian Monarchy or for the German nation. The last Balkan War
was more disastrous for Panslavism than the first one was for Turkey."

Byron, Canning, and Gladstone; of Napoleon III and Gambetta; of Diebitsch and Skobeloff. The results of a century of national striving would be swept away in order that the Teutons might force their way to the East. It is in face of such an issue that Greece, the first-born of Europe's children, vacillates, while Bulgaria, the youngest of the family, has foully betrayed the Slavonic national cause to which she owes her very existence.

Such are the crucial developments of Nationalism since the year 1885. The revival of racial feuds in the Balkans at that time ensured the triumph of the barbarous policy of Abdul Hamid, which continued to desolate Macedonia and Armenia until 1908. The accession of Wilhelm II in 1888 inaugurated an era of aggressive Nationalism in Germany and, somewhat later, in Austria, the result being Pangermanism and its varied efforts which culminated in July, 1914. After the accession of the Tsar Nicholas II in 1894 the diversion of Russia's energies towards the Far East emasculated the Panslav movement, so powerful under his predecessors; and Slavonic sentiment retained its vitality chiefly among the Serbs and other South Slavs, who could not effect much. The growth of Pangermanism and its alliance with the Turks and the Panislam movement has proved to be the chief determining factor in recent history. That these national movements have developed immense energies in their respective peoples admits of no doubt; but the events of 1914-5 form the supreme test as to the worth of the new Nationalism.

LECTURE X

INTERNATIONALISM

"Si une guerre menace d'éclater, c'est un devoir de la classe
ouvrière dans les pays concernés, c'est un devoir pour leurs repré-
sentants dans les Parlements, avec l'aide du bureau international,
force d'action et de co-ordination, de faire tous leurs efforts pour
empêcher la guerre. . . ."—Resolution of the Congress of l'Internationale at Stuttgart, August, 1907.

PERIODS of war and peace succeed each other with a per-
sistence which must arouse the curiosity of every well-wisher
of mankind. Unless we accept Bernhardi's view (now so
popular in Germany) that war is a necessary school of the
manly virtues, its periodicity is a distressing symptom.
Certainly, those who believe that human progress is advanced
more by peace will continue to inquire whether means of
avoiding conflicts may not be discovered and successfully
applied. I will try here to review this question in the light
of the teachings of history.

Inquiries of this kind have been especially numerous at
the end of long and devastating campaigns; and it is not
too much to say that efforts in favor of peace and legality
have been in proportion to the horrors of warfare.

This truth is obvious in the case of the founder of International Law, Hugo van Groot (Grotius). Living amidst
the atrocities that disgraced the Wars of Religion, that
Dutch scholar pondered over the utter lawlessness that had
of late afflicted mankind. In words that might now be written
by a Belgian, Pole, or Serb, Grotius in 1625 thus set forth
his reason for inculcating the principles of public right:

"I saw prevailing throughout the Christian world a licence
in making war of which even barbarous nations would have
been ashamed, recourse being had to arms for slight reason
or no reason; and, when arms were once taken up, all reverence for divine and human law was then thrown away, just
as if men were henceforth authorized to commit all crimes
without restraint." [1] The subsequent atrocities of the Thirty
Years' War emphasized the need for some guiding and restraining authority; and hence by degrees there grew up a
code of public law, the chief contributors to which (like the
German Pufendorf in 1661) were those who had experienced
the terrors of lawlessness. In 1693, during our campaigns
against Louis XIV, the Quaker, William Penn, set forth
proposals for the preservation of peace; and in 1713, at
the end of the War of the Spanish Succession, the French
priest, Charles de St. Pierre, drew up a scheme which I shall
notice presently. As the din of arms filled the greater part
of the eighteenth century, thinkers occupied themselves
with the problems of war and peace. Voltaire, Montesquieu,
and Rousseau in France;[2] Adam Smith and the younger
Pitt in England; Kant and Lessing in Germany, all voiced
the pacific aspirations of the age. The French *Economistes*
and Adam Smith advocated principles which would have
transformed the Continental States into friendly economic
units among a comity of nations.

Especially noteworthy were the efforts of German thinkers

[1] Quoted by Dr. T. J. Lawrence, *The Principles of International Law*,
p. 42. I omit Henri IV's peace project as unimportant.

[2] Again it is worth noting that the books which dealt heavy blows at
the warlike ambitions and false aims of the *ancien régime* appeared at
or near the end of wars, e. g. *Les Lettres persanes* (1721), *L'Esprit des
Lois* (1748), *L'Encyclopédie* (1751–65), *Le Contrat social* (1762), *Le
Système de la Nature* (1770). As I have shown in my *Life of Pitt* (I,
p. 340), William Pulteney in 1786 proposed to Pitt a plan of arbitration,
and Pitt's treaty with France of that year was an effort for lasting peace.

on behalf of peace and brotherhood. The philosophical movement in France found a clear echo across the Rhine, where leading men desired to end racial rivalries. Deeming patriotism a promoter of strife, they belittled that instinct. The genial Lessing wrote: "I have no conception of the love of country; and it seems to me at best a heroic failing, which I am well content to be without." Indeed he aspired to a far higher ideal. In his most perfect play, *Nathan der Weise* (1779), the hero is a Jewish merchant of the time of Saladin, who, even in that time of bigotry, disarms racial and religious hatreds by the attractive power of goodness. Rivalries vanish before the magic of his virtue; and the play ends with a spectacle of concord and happiness. Lessing took the leading incident of the play from Boccaccio; but he transformed the story by investing it with the ethical promise of his own time, the Age of Enlightenment.

Kant enforced similar precepts in his tractate *Perpetual Peace*, published in 1795 shortly after Prussia came to terms with France in the Peace of Basel. He proposed as the chief step towards peace a Federation of free States. They must be Republics, i. e. they must be States endowed with really representative institutions—which would rule out all forms of Bonapartism with their modern equivalent, Kaiserism.[1] These free States would form definite compacts one with the other, thus laying the foundation for a system of International Law, binding on all, and thereby substituting the reign of right for merely national aims. Just as individuals had by degrees consented to give up something of their entire liberty so as to secure order, similarly (he urged) it ought to be possible to substitute some measure of international control for that extreme ideal of national liberty which often led to war. Kant was not very hopeful

[1] Kant, *Perpetual Peace* (Eng. Transl. by M. Campbell, Smith), p. 123.

on this score. He saw that for nations to give up their natural
liberty (including the liberty to expand and to make war)
implied an immense advance in ethical ideas, as is now painfully obvious. Further, in his *Rechtslehre*, he stated that
mankind can arrive at permanent peace "only in a universal
Union of States, by a process analogous to that through which
a people becomes a State. Since, however, the too great
extension of such a State of Nations over vast territories
must, in the long run, render impossible the government of
that Union—and therefore the protection of each of its
members—a multitude of such corporations will again lead
to a state of war. So that perpetual peace, the final goal of
international law, as a whole, is really an impracticable
idea." Nevertheless, he hoped that these political principles
might approximate towards that end.

For my part I do not admit that the extension of the area
of these federating States is an objection to Kant's theory.
His fear on this topic was, I believe, grounded on the objection felt by him, by Rousseau, and by all his contemporaries, to the formation of great realms. They all held
that civil liberty was incompatible with great States and
could be attained and retained only in small communities.
The fear was very natural in times of slow and difficult
communications. It is groundless now in the days of railways
and telegraphs; and in that respect we are far more favor-
ably situated than our forefathers for building up a great
Union of States. Indeed, it is essential that such a Union
or Federation should comprise practically all the great States.
It is not too great an extension, but too partial an extension,
that is the danger. As we have recently seen, there is no
security for peace so long as one great nation remains outside the circle of those that desire peace.

Further, if any great State comes into such a Union with
the notion of being the leader, that Union will be a sham and

a delusion. Not until the federating States, one and all, put far from them the idea of predominance, will there be a reasonable hope of securing fair play, justice, and therefore peace. Kant saw this clearly, and therefore stipulated that there must be a "universal will determining the rights and property of each individual nation"; and this universal will (an extension of Rousseau's "general will" of a single community) must take the form of a contract.[1]

Let us look at this question by the light of experience. In 1713, at the end of the War of the Spanish Succession, l'Abbé de St. Pierre published a tractate on peace. His chief contentions were that Christendom should combine to form a federation of States under the lead of France, and proceed, as the first of its pacific duties, to turn the Turks out of Europe. These proposals sufficed to damn the scheme as a device for re-establishing French prestige recently shattered by Marlborough.

Not very dissimilar was a scheme of Napoleon I. During his sojourn at St. Helena (which ought to have cured him of his notions of world-supremacy) the illustrious exile described his plan of forming the European Association. He would have imposed the same system, the same principles everywhere, the same Code of Laws, a Supreme Tribunal, the same weights and measures, a similar coinage, so that Europe would have formed but one people. But it is significant that all these plans were closely connected in his mind with the conquest of Russia. That implied in his mind the "beginning of security"; and then only could the European System be founded. Thereafter he would have his Congress to settle Europe; also his Holy Alliance.[2]

[1] Kant, App. II, § 2.
[2] Las Cases, *Mémorial de Ste. Hélène* (B, 398–400), (August, 1816). So, too, he told Count Rambuteau (*Mémoires*, p. 55, Eng. edit.) that his

In much the same spirit the German Chancellor, Beth-mann-Hollweg, said to the Reichstag on August 19, 1915: "If Europe is to come to peace, it can only be possible by the inviolable and strong position of Germany. The English policy of the Balance of Power must disappear." These words imply that Germany will not accept a position of mere equality of power; she must be supreme. The claim is not urged with the extravagance that characterized Napoleon's final regrets. Nevertheless, the German claim to supremacy is absolutely incompatible with the principle of proportionate equality on which alone a federation of free States can be firmly established. Minds of a certain bent cannot conceive of any other way of imposing order and quiet than that of enforcement by some superior Power. Well! It cannot be too clearly understood that that way lies war. For, sooner or later, your constabulary guardian will develop into a drill sergeant; and thence must ensue the rule of force and therefore strife. I grant that the drill sergeant theory is the simpler; and very many people can understand no other way. They cannot see that harmony attained by the agreement of all is infinitely preferable to, and more probably lasting than, a harmony produced by dread of a superior.

Let us, however, frankly confess that a union of peoples on proportionate terms is difficult to attain and still more difficult to maintain. The French Revolution egregiously failed in the international sphere. Though it began with the profession of fraternity, yet its practice degenerated under the strain of war. Military considerations, backed up by national pride, carried the day at Paris; and French democracy, even before the rise of Bonaparte, was committed to courses directly opposed to the cosmopolitan aims of 1789. It was a German thinker who in 1795 pointed

Empire would be safe only when he was master of all the capitals of Europe.

towards peace, while France headed towards wider conquests
—and Bonapartism.

The efforts of the Tsar Alexander I in and after 1815 to
promote a Confederation of Europe need not detain us long.
There prevailed then a general desire for peace, one expression of which was the founding of the Peace Society in London
in 1816.[1] Whether Alexander had more in view an Association of Peoples on equal terms or a Confederation of States
more or less under his direction cannot be discussed here.
Certain it is that, if ever he cherished the lofty views ascribed
to him in 1815, they soon vanished; and the promised federation of the European peoples became a mere device for
depriving them of political and civic liberty. The period of
the Congresses (1818–22) therefore merits the sarcastic cen-
sure which Sorel applies to International Law, that it was
known "only through the declamations of publicists and its
violation by the Governments." It is not surprising that all
students of that disappointing era should view with reserve
and suspicion all proposals for World-Tribunals and International Congresses. But the optimist may reply: "Both
the men and the methods were defective. The men were
autocrats and were easily turned aside into reactionary
paths." This is undeniable; and I refuse to believe that,
because Metternich lured Alexander aside, therefore Congresses of delegates chosen for the purpose of founding a
Union of European States need necessarily be held in vain.
We have nearly a hundred years of experience behind us
since Aix-la-Chapelle and Verona. I trust that, after the
present war, we shall have before us principles more definite
and sound than that of "morality based on bayonets," which
aptly summarizes the bastard Internationalism of 1818–22.

[1] I have no space in which to notice the works of Gentz, l'Abbé de
Pradt, etc. See Pradt's *L'Europe après le Congrès*, and Alison Phillips'
Confederation of Empire.

It is, however, instructive to notice the extreme ease with which the philanthropic views of the Tsar were perverted; and the experience of those years bids us beware of benevolent doctrinaires no less than wily diplomats. The dreamer is as dangerous as his first cousin, the trickster, into whose hands he frequently plays.

More genuine than the federalism of the Tsar Alexander were the aims of Mazzini and the Young Europe Movement of 1834–5 by which he sought to group together the democrats of Italy, France, and Switzerland, as well as other peoples. The sporadic movements of 1830 having failed owing to utter lack of concert, Mazzini now sought to co-ordinate them. By means of a central advisory body in Switzerland he endeavored to form what he called a "college of intellects," which would both incite and guide democrats of various lands. But that movement failed, largely because its lofty aims appealed only to groups of intellectuals. The generation that grew up under Napoleon and his conquerors was too exhausted to rise in revolt until the hardships of 1847–8 reinforced the teachings of idealists. As Lord Acton observed, Mazzini's conspiracy was founded not on a grievance but "on a doctrine"; [1] and the experiences of 1848 were to show that the doctrines must be practical and the grievances intense to produce unanimity among peoples only half awakened. "Young Europe" virtually collapsed with Mazzini's removal to London in 1837; and it is questionable whether the exiles who founded "Young Europe," or the fiercer group of Panslavists that gyrated around Bakunin in Paris in 1847, had any practical influence on the democratic movements of 1848–9.

The events of those luckless years showed the extreme difficulty of Democracy and Nationality working well together, and justify the belief that they are in their nature opposed. Wherever the fervid nationalists got the upper

[1] Lord Acton, *Essays on Liberty*, p. 286.

hand, liberty was jealously restricted to the leading race; and as a result there prevailed those cries: "Hungary for the Hungarians," etc., which brought Nationalism into deserved disrepute. In Italy alone were the democrats inspired by broader views, thanks to the inspiring influence of Mazzini; but at Rome and Venice the foreigner stamped out both Nationalism and Democracy, so that by the end of 1849 the future of the Continent was most dreary. In his essay *Europe: its Condition* (1852) Mazzini pointed out that Europe no longer believed in the Papacy, or in dynasties or aristocracies. In fact Europe possessed no unity of aim, of faith, or of mission. But, he proceeded, a new initiative would probably arise out of the question of nationalities, which would destroy the Treaties of Vienna and assort the peoples in accord with their desires. "The question of nationalities (he wrote), rightly understood, is the alliance of the peoples, the balance of powers based on new foundations, the organization of the work that Europe has to accomplish." At that time such a solution was possible. The peoples were not yet at enmity; and they all had an interest in striving for more complete self-expression, firstly, by becoming complete political entities instead of remaining divided fragments; secondly, by solving the social and industrial problems in a way that was impossible in their then fragmentary existence. Alas! the nations did not rearrange their political boundaries without strifes that left behind rankling hatreds; and in consequence the social and industrial problems have gone unsolved. Nationalism asserted itself in its cruder form, clothed itself in Militarism, and made the Continent a series of self-contained and hostile nations.

Consequently, the international movement, which concurrently struggled for recognition, had little chance of success. Its beginnings may be traced in the famous Association called *l'Internationale,* which was started by French and British workmen in London in 1864. Originating in meetings of French working-men visitors to our Exhibition of 1862 with our own artisans, it soon had branches in all countries; and at its Congresses revolutionary Socialism of the most advanced type gained ground. The anarchic section got the upper hand in 1869, when Bakunin and his Russian and Polish Nihilists joined the Association. Its influence on the Paris Commune of 1871 has been disputed, but I think on insufficient grounds. M. Hanotaux estimates the number of its members in Paris at between 70,000 and 80,000, and thinks that Bismarck may have encouraged the anarchic propaganda of the French Communists. The idea may seem far-fetched; but Bismarck was a past master in the art of weakening his enemies; and, on January 27, 1871, during an interview with Jules Favre, he alluded to the dangerous state of public opinion in Paris on the eve of its surrender to the Germans, and gave the following Machiavellian advice: "Provoke an *émeute* while you still have an army to suppress it with." [1] Favre looked at him with horror, for making so bloodthirsty a suggestion. But evidently Bismarck knew the state of things in Paris better than Favre, who, later on, probably regretted that he did not follow that cunning counsel.

The *Internationale* played Germany's game admirably in completing the ruin of France in the spring of 1871, when Lyons and other cities of the Centre and South sought to copy Paris and overturn the national Government. In its place they sought to erect a system based on the Commune as governing unit, with federations to endow these microcosms with some solidarity. That the Communists should have made their bold bid for power while France was still writhing under the heel of the Germans sufficiently characterized their movement. It proved that among a fanatical

[1] Busch, *Bismarck during the Franco-German War*, II, 265.

minority of "Internationals" all claims of country were ignored; nay, that the greater the agony of *la patrie*, the better was the opportunity deemed for sweeping away old-world notions and imposing a communistic and anti-national form of society. Of course the national view prevailed, but after a terrible struggle, which brought France to the verge of dissolution. The violence of the *pétroleuses* in Paris and other signs of political lunacy discredited the cause; and in 1872 the *Internationale* split into two factions. The more moderate, led by Marx, outvoted the desperadoes of Bakunin; but the latter found a considerable following among the artisans of France, and, still more, of Spain and Italy. Worsted at their own game of violence, the Nihilists gradually declined in numbers; but the Russian branch of the sect effected the murder of the reforming Tsar, Alexander II, and thus threw Russia into the arms of reaction.

The chief significance of these facts lies in the reckless unwisdom of the champions of Internationalism and their utter disregard of the claims of country, even after a most disastrous war; but it is of prime importance to observe that anarchic and anti-national theories had a far greater hold on the Slav and Latin peoples than on the Germans. The Karl Marx party dominant in German Socialism, though advanced in its opinions, was not anarchic. Indeed, Marx often behaved like a German patriot. On July 20, 1870, just before the Franco-German War, he wrote to another Socialist, Engels, that he hoped the French would be well thrashed; then the centre of the *Internationale* would be in Germany. He was no less hostile to the French Republic. On the contrary, Bakunin did his best to help the young French democracy against the Germans.[1] Thus, the Teutonic Socialist tended towards Nationalism, the French and Rus-

[1] James Guillaume, *Karl Marx pangermaniste, et l'Association Internationale* (Paris, Colin, 1915), pp. 85, 101.

sians towards Internationalism; the fractions that now and
again terrorized the Latin and Russian peoples were the declared enemies, not only of those Governments, but of all
government.

This divergence between the Teutonic peoples on the one
hand and the Latin and Slav peoples on the other suggests
that there must be a fundamental difference of temperament and outlook. In the Latin and Slav peoples the sense
of the ideal is certainly stronger; and the notion of a common
law and civilization has taken deeper root. Consequently,
on every important question the authority of the community
tends to prevail—a heritage bequeathed in rich measure by
Ancient Rome to the Romance peoples. The Slav peoples
are characterized by similar notions, and by an even stronger
vein of sentiment. Consequently a movement that aims at
far-reaching changes, such as the sovereignty of the community or of the human race at large over the individual, has a
greater chance of success among them than elsewhere. In
fact, far-reaching social revolutions have generally originated with them. On the other hand the Germanic, Anglo-
Saxon, and Scandinavian peoples are remarkable for attachment to the home and to individual liberty. Luther and
Cromwell are their characteristic products; Rousseau and
Mazzini those of the Latin peoples. Accordingly, it seems
probable that Internationalism will develop first among the
latter, and will be retarded by the individualism of the former.

However, in 1871 the movement was wrecked mainly by
the extravagant ardor of its disciples. Mrs. Browning has
sung of the proneness of the French of her day to hurry to
extremes:—

> "these too fiery and impatient souls,
> They threaten conflagration to the world,
> And rush with most unscrupulous logic on
> Impossible practice."

Never was this defect more flagrant than in the spring of 1871. It was due to the Communists that the French Republic became for a time a prey to reaction. In Germany, on the contrary, the anarchist movement never was serious; and the majority of the Socialists in the long run tended to express not much more than the discontent naturally aroused by the autocratic proceedings of the present Kaiser. Even the Marxian Socialists have diminished in Germany, where, indeed, the Socialists are often little more than upholders of individual liberty. During the first seven or eight years of his reign William II sought to appease them by measures known as State Socialism: but in and after 1895 he found that his imperial palliatives were not appreciated, and in 1896 he threw himself into *Weltpolitik*.

As we have seen, this commercial Imperialism gained ground rapidly; and, what is most remarkable, it won over very many German Socialists. The reasons for their defection are still far from clear; but one cause, perhaps the fundamental cause, has been pointed out by a Belgian, M. Émile Royer. He, the Socialist deputy for Tournay, states that Marxism had devoted itself almost exclusively to the national side of social questions, thereby losing sight of the wider and humanitarian issues which nerved the Socialists of 1848.[1] This explanation goes far to solve the riddle; for since the year 1888 the German Government has done much for the workmen, and recently has tried to convince them of the need of colonies and better outlets to the sea. To men who looked chiefly to the loaves and fishes the Kaiser's policy presented irresistible attractions. For instance, the Pangerman programme, which he patronized, has aimed at the inclusion of Belgium and Holland in a Greater Germany—to which a

[1] *Indépendance belge*, Feb. 17, 1915; quoted by J. Destrée, *Les Socialistes el la Guerre européenne*, p. 20.

Central Zollverein would be the convenient prelude; and this programme has immensely furthered the growth of imperial and Chauvinistic ideas among the Bavarians. Shedding their former separatist notions, they have embraced the new programme with ardor, because, as their King recently stated, it promises to give to South German trade its natural outlets to the sea, Rotterdam and Antwerp. Similarly in the great commercial centres, very many Socialists have favored the imperial policy of expansion.

Their conduct has dealt a heavy blow to the international cause. Most of the fathers of Socialism believed in Free Trade between nations as a means of furthering friendly intercourse and lessening the chances of war. But Bismarck's policy of protecting home industries (supplemented by that of Bülow respecting agriculture) had very important results, far beyond the limits of commerce and agriculture. For there were two alternatives before Germany; either to continue in the path of Free Trade, which implies peaceful intercourse, or to adopt a protective and narrowly national policy. Bismarck chose the latter, and Wilhelm accentuated the choice, his aim being to make the nation as far as possible a self-sufficing unit. The result was that Germany in forty years of peace piled up great stores of industrial energy which threatened to burst their bounds. On the basis of protection vast industrial interests were built up, which could find no adequate markets unless other States let in German goods on easy terms; and this they would not do to a sufficient extent. Consequently the national or protective system led to an impasse. The new trade interests clamored for new markets, and the artisans concerned in them tended to become imperial expansionists. Thus the protective system adopted in 1880 served to strengthen the demands for further annexations.

In fact the whole system gyrated in a vicious circle, somewhat as follows: First the colonial party demanded colonies and protection. Then the colonies were stated to need a great fleet; while protection led to a mushroom growth of industries which helped to pay for the fleet. Industries, inflated to near bursting point, demanded new outlets, and all classes of the community, including many of the Socialists, believed it necessary to support that demand, which the army and fleet were prepared to satisfy. If Germany had persevered with the system of free exchange which makes the whole world an open market, the present cataclysm would probably have been averted; for though the Prussian Junkers would in any case clamor for war, their cries would have found no response in commercial circles, still less among the artisans of Germany. These last, I repeat, have been largely led astray from international ideals by a narrow commercialism, which made either for an internal explosion or a European war. In these islands we think of commerce as a bond of peace. It has acted far otherwise in Germany, where it takes on the guise of the old mercantile system, that fruitful parent of wars in the seventeenth and eighteenth centuries. Indeed, over-speculation and over-production in Germany probably prompted the mad plunge of July, 1914.[1] Antwerp, Salonica, Constantinople, and Bagdad were to be the safety-valves for a surcharged industrial system. The conquest of Belgium and North-East France, Poland, Courland, and the Balkans seemed no difficult task in view of the confusion and weakness in the Entente States and Serbia. Commerce therefore joined hands with Militarism, and German Socialists did not bestow on that suspicious union the expected shower of curses.

Imperialism, of course, has sometimes assumed a threatening guise in these islands; but on the whole it has aimed at

[1] See M. Millioud, *The Ruling Caste and Frenzied Trade in Germany* (Eng. transl., 1916).

safeguarding the Empire by the upkeep of an adequate fleet, the increase of which barely kept pace with that of the mercantile marine and of our colonial responsibilities. The rôle of the British fleet was necessarily defensive; that of the German fleet, on its very limited coasts, could, after the recent huge additions, well be offensive. In truth, the danger of the situation lay in the fact that the greatest military Power in the world aspired to rival on the oceans the Power for which maritime supremacy is the first law of existence. This difference in the situation of Germany and Great Britain was never admitted by the German people; and of late years their Socialists have ceased effectively to protest against the increase of their armaments, and that, too, despite the persistent refusal of the Berlin Government to accept proposals at the Hague Conferences for limitation of armaments.[1]

In view of the inaction of German Socialists at the greatest crisis in the modern world, it is of interest to glance at the resolutions which their delegates helped to pass at the chief Congresses of the *Internationale*. At Paris in 1901 the Congress engaged the Socialists of all countries to oppose votes for naval construction and colonial wars. At Stuttgart in 1907 that able French writer, Gustave Hervé, spoke vehemently against patriotism as an anti-social prejudice. The German leader, Bebel, opposed this on the ground that *la patrie* belongs more to the poor than to the dominant classes; and he warned Hervé not to encourage the German General Staff against "the eventual enemy." For himself, he would not support war, but he supported defensive preparations. Hervé, in reply, said that his propaganda in France

[1] Bernhardi's claim, that Germany needs new colonies for her surplus population, is refuted by the official statement in the *Preussische Jahrbücher* of March, 1912, that her emigration had of late sunk to about 20,000 a year.

had disarmed the Government, which in case of mobilization, would be faced with insurrection and chaos. Bebel declared that there were two million Socialists in the German army, but gave no promise as to their conduct in case of a war, which, moreover, would further their cause better than ten years of propaganda. The Congress unanimously voted a motion, the chief clause of which appears at the head of this lecture.

The Congress held at Copenhagen in 1910 rejected Keir Hardie's motion for a general strike of workers in case of war by 131 votes to 51. In the majority were Germany 20 votes, Austria 18, Italy 15, America 14, etc.; in the minority, Great Britain 20, France 12, Russia 7, Poland 5, etc. The delegates who met at the Bâle Congress of November, 1912, were cheered by the sweeping triumphs of the party in the recent General Elections to the Reichstag (see *ante*, p. 191). Referring to the Balkan War then raging, the French leader, Jaurès, called on the workers in Germany, France, and England to prevent any help going to Austria or Russia if those Powers came to blows. The German delegate, Hasse, for his party, promised to use all possible means to prevent a war.[1]

A sinister incident followed. In the hope of clearing up the Alsace-Lorraine Question 180 French Socialists went on to Berne, expecting to meet the same number of German delegates. They found a mere handful; for as one of them said to M. Vergnet: "Every German, from the highest to the lowest, considers that the Alsace-Lorraine Question can be reopened only on the battlefield. Let the French have no illusion on that head." [2] The German Socialists also made no sustained protests against the barbarous treat-

[1] E. Royer, *La Social-Démocratie allemande et austro-hongroise et les Socialistes belges*, pp. 8-24. (17-18 Green St., Leicester Square, London).

[2] Vergnet, *The German Engima*, p. 138.

ment of certain harmless civilians of Zabern by German officers near the close of 1913. At that time the centenary celebrations of the German War of Liberation of 1813 turned all heads in the Fatherland; and Germany, though she had no Napoleon to fear, whipped herself to a frenzy of warlike ardor, amidst which the 110 Socialist members of the Reichstag raised scarcely a protest against the enormous votes passed in that autumn for military and naval purposes—votes which far exceeded all possible demands of a defensive character. Thereafter the Berlin Government was convinced that in any eventuality the German Socialists would (to use a famous phrase of Bebel's) "fight to the last gasp for the Fatherland." Of course, the great Socialist had spoken thus only for a really defensive war. In July-August, 1914, his party condoned the action of the German Government when it precipitated the long-dreaded European conflict.

Here it is well to recall the condition of Labor in the chief countries. The spring and summer of 1914 were characterized by great unrest in France, Great Britain, and Russia. Strikes were numerous and others were threatened. Frequent ministerial crises at Paris and public admissions as to the unpreparedness of the army weakened public confidence. As for the United Kingdom, it seemed on the verge of civil war in Ireland. In Russia the strikes of the transport workers and others opened up the most serious prospects. It was in this state of affairs, when the Entente Powers hovered on the brink of social revolution or civil war, that Germany launched her ultimatums to Petrograd and Paris (July 31). Those acts alone, following on the insolent demands of the Austrian Government on Serbia, sufficiently revealed the aggressive designs of the Central Empires, which became clear as day when Germany sought to "hew her way" through Belgium.

It is curious that, in the early stages of the diplomatic

quarrel, the German Socialists raised protests against being dragged into war. On July 28 they held twenty-eight public meetings in Berlin alone for that purpose; and those meetings were even protected by the police. This fact seems to show that either the authorities had not yet decided in favor of war (it is thought that they decided on the evening of July 29) or that they were using the Socialists to lull those of Russia, France, and Belgium into false security. In either case the opposition of German Socialists to war thenceforth collapsed—why is a mystery. Were they coerced by the officials? Or were they terrified by the Muscovite bogey which Berlin officials magnified into colossal proportions? The latter supposition is incredible in view of the almost complete paralysis of the transport services in Russia. It seems, then, that the German Socialists must have followed the imperialist impulse which had won them over in and after the year 1912. Whatever the cause, they all (though a few silently demurred) supported the war votes of August 4 for a campaign which a mere tyro in diplomacy could see was of an offensive character. Nevertheless, Hasse read out the Socialists' declaration that they no longer had to pronounce on the cause of the war, but only to defend their frontiers; and on this wretched excuse he and his party gave the lie to their protestations of several years past. His action was all the more disgraceful because on July 29, at a great meeting of Socialists at Brussels, he declared Austria's demands on Serbia a veritable provocation to war, and affirmed the conviction of the German people that its Government ought not to intervene, even if Russia intervened. It was then decided to hold a great International Congress at Paris on August 9 to concert general measures to prevent war.[1] Did the knowledge of that fact induce the Berlin

---

[1] Royer, pp. 24–31: P. G. la Chesnais, "The Socialist Party in the Reichstag and the Declaration of War," ch. 3, shows that that party

Government to hurry on its ultimatums to Russia and France on July 31? And why did not those obvious signs of hurry arouse the suspicions of the 110 Socialist deputies? Why, during the sitting of August 4th, did they not protest against the violation of Belgium's neutrality, which the Chancellor admitted to be a lawless act? Why, finally, did they not protest against the horrors perpetrated in Belgium in August-September?

In justice, it must be said that the Socialist journal, the *Vorwärts*, protested both against the war and the barbarities of the army. Liebknecht, too, in December, 1914, in opposing the second war credits, declared the war to be an imperialist and capitalist war for the conquest of the world's markets. By that time all German Socialists were aware of the absolute preparedness of Germany and the unpreparedness of her opponents. Yet only sixteen Socialist deputies joined in his opposition and protest. By degrees his following increased; and the majority of the German Socialist party has finally condemned the policy of annexation openly avowed in the time of fancied triumph. Some of its members, however, sought to persuade their French and Belgian comrades that France and Belgium ought to discuss terms of peace. Against this suggestion Bernstein, editor of the *Bremer Bürgerzeitung*, strongly protested, pointing out that, as France was attacked and part of her territory still occupied, discussions of peace by her would be a fatal act. Bernstein, Liebknecht, Kautzky, and Hasse published a Socialist manifesto demanding peace, without annexations

---

abandoned all opposition to war in its manifesto of July 31, *that is before war became certain.* The *Vorwärts* also wrote: "Social Democracy bears no responsibility for forthcoming events"—a forecast of the passivity of the party on August 4. On August 1 a German Socialist, Müller, arrived at Paris, and sought to induce his French comrades to oppose the war credits at Paris.

or conquests.   They and their manifesto were repudiated by the party, which thus associated itself with the policy of the Government (June, 1915).[1]

As for the French Socialists, though stunned for a moment by the assassination of their leader, Jaurès, they soon took up the position which, assuredly, he would have taken up. In face of the unprovoked and treacherous stab of the Germans at France through Belgium, they rallied as one man to the defence of *la patrie*. There was now no talk of a "general strike" such as might conceivably have stopped the war at its two sources, Berlin and Vienna. The treason of German Socialists to the *Internationale* consigned it for the present to the limbo of vain hopes; and nothing remained for their comrades in Belgium, France, Serbia, and Poland but to fall back on the old principle of duty to their several nations. The supreme lesson of the crisis of July-August, 1914, is that Internationalism can succeed only when its votaries stand firm in every nation; and that treason in one quarter involves collapse in all quarters.

The genius of the Latin and Slav peoples was quick to discern the truth that in August, 1914, the patriotic principle, which many of them had consistently derided, formed the only possible basis of action during the war; also that, in fighting for *la patrie* against its violators, they were taking the first step towards reaffirming the cosmopolitan ideal. Very noteworthy was the action of Gustave Hervé. He at once became a flaming patriot, the champion of war to the

---

[1] Destrée, pp. 17, 35–46.   H. Bourgin, *Les Responsabilités du Social-isme allemand*, pp. 14–22.   The assertion of Mr. Snowden, m. p., in the debate of February 23, 1916, that in no country of Europe (except Hungary and Italy) has Internationalism been so well kept alive as by the German Socialists, is incorrect.   They have made some fine speeches, but their actions have been timid and far too tardy to influ-ence events, except in a sense favorable to Germany.

death against Germany. The Belgian Socialist, Destrée, by his fiery denunciation of the Huns, did much to arouse Italy from her indecision and range her on the side of national liberty against an overweening Imperialism. In Great Britain the action of the workers has in general been marked by self-sacrificing devotion; but unfortunately one section of the Labor party has been blind to the wider issues at stake in this mighty struggle. Consequently there has not been here that unanimous rally to the nation's call which has lifted the whole life of France to a higher level. In France, despite a sharp rise in prices, there has not been a single strike since the beginning of the war up to mid-February, 1916; but here as many as 698 strikes occurred during the year 1915 alone. Of these several were due to merely local and sectional considerations, and many were highly detrimental to the public service. The contrast is deeply humiliating, and is not to be explained away by saying that France is invaded and we are not; for the same principle, the freedom of the smaller peoples, is at stake everywhere. Inability or refusal to see this truth must discredit a portion of the British Labor party; and leadership in the international movement of the future will probably lie with the Latin or Slav peoples, whose workers have almost unanimously shown the capacity of taking a wide, generous, and statesmanlike view of this unexampled crisis in the fortunes of the European peoples.

In Russia the Socialists were at first divided on the question of the war, as was natural in view of the despotic nature of their Government. But their leaders, notably Prince Kropotkin, soon perceived the seriousness of the German menace; and the party rallied enthusiastically to the national cause. At the International Socialist Congress held in London in February, 1915, all the Russian delegates voted for the prosecution of the war until the rights of nationalities were restored and a federative system could be designed for the protection of the peace of Europe.

That has become the aim of nearly all Socialists in this war; but, in spite of the increase of distress in Germany, her Socialist party continues to support the Government. In a debate early in January, 1916, Liebknecht's anti-war group mustered forty-one strong; but the refusal of the German Chancellor to repudiate aims of annexation on either frontier failed to alienate the majority of the Socialists. For their part, the French Socialists demand that the future of Alsace-Lorraine shall be decided by a plébiscite in those provinces, a proposal scouted by their German *confrères*, who claim that that future is irrevocably bound up with German rule. On this rock, then, as well as that of Poland, Internationalism has foundered; and it will be observed that, while its ideal is championed by French and Russian Socialists, those of Germany have in the main taken up the nationalist standpoint and hold to the lands seized or conquered by Frederick the Great and Wilhelm I.[1] In January, 1916, the Socialist leader, Scheidemann, spoke strongly for peace and against annexations; but he uttered the fatal words: "We refuse any thought of an annexation of Alsace-Lorraine by France, in whatever form it may be attempted."

Another blow to the cosmopolitan movement is the utter failure of neutrals to give effect to their obligations, contracted at the Hague Conferences, for assuring the sanctity of neutral territory and the rights due to non-combatants. Though Germany's weaker neighbors were obviously terrorized into silence, yet the United States could safely have protested in the case of outrages so notorious as those committed in Belgium and Poland. No protest has come from

[1] See the *Temps* for Nov. 6, 1915, and the *Nation* (London) or Jan. 15, 1916.

Washington;[1] and this dereliction of duty has rendered futile all the labor expended at the Hague Conferences, at least during this war. Here again, then, experience has proved the extreme fragility of the cosmopolitan ideals. At the first contact with a brutal and overweening Nationalism they vanished; and Germany has plunged the world back into a state of lawlessness and bestiality comparable with that of the Thirty Years' War.

Men are asking everywhere: Can International Law and morality ever be re-established in such a way as to restore confidence? Pessimists and cynics deny it. On historical grounds, I dissent from this sombre estimate. For, as has appeared in these studies, Nationalism shows signs of having exhausted its strength except among the most backward peoples. This war is the *reductio ad absurdum* of the movement in its recent narrow and intolerant form. The persistent attempt of one nation to overbear its weaker neighbors in order to achieve world-supremacy has sufficed to unite against it nearly all the world; and the frightful exhaustion which failure must entail will be a warning to would-be world-conquerors for centuries to come. Further, as we have seen, the more brutal and perfidious the violation of International Law, the stronger is the demand for the re-establishment of that law, with adequate guarantees for the future. In the domains of politics, finance, and law violent action always begets a strong reaction; and we may be sure that, when the base Nationalism of recent years has brought its protagonist to ruin, there will be a potent revulsion in favor of international ideals. In 1871 those ideals were foolishly championed

[1] In his Allocution of January 22, 1915, the Pope reprobated all acts of injustice, but in terms so general as to render the protest useless. Equally disappointing is the letter of Cardinal Gasparri, of July 6, 1915, to the Belgian Minister (*L'Allemagne et les Alliés devant la Conscience chrétienne, ad fin.*, Paris, 1915).

by the fanatics of Paris; in 1914 they were foully betrayed by turncoats at Berlin. Let us hope that in the future good sense and good faith will work hand in hand for their realization. Already in the Hague Tribunal there exists the means for assuring the triumph of reason in place of force. If in due course *all* the European Powers consent to substitute the will to reconcile for the will to conquer, the task is half accomplished.

Why should not the new Europe will to reconcile its interests? Every leading thinker now admits that the saner of the national aspirations (that is, those which prompt the political union of men of like sentiments) must receive due satisfaction. Belgium will be reconstituted, more glorious than before. France must recover Alsace-Lorraine. But the French and Belgian peoples, if they are wise, will not covet the Rhine boundary. Poland (the Poland of 1771) ought to emerge once more, free in civic affairs, though under the suzerainty of the Tsars. Italy will gather in her people of the Trentino and Trieste, but, if she is wise, will annex no Slovene or Slav lands further east. The Austrian and Eastern Questions are more difficult, but can be settled on a federative system based on Nationality and equality of rights. The Macedonian tangle should be settled by a commission appointed by the Great Powers, not by wrangling delegates of the peoples concerned. On the questions concerning Albania, Bulgaria, and Constantinople no prudent person will at present dogmatize; for they must be settled largely according to the course of events. This much is certain: the enormous importance of the issues now at stake ought to nerve every Briton to do his utmost so that the solution shall be thorough and shall not end in the ghastly fiasco of a stale-mate. Better five years of war than that.

The new Europe which I have outlined ought to be a far

happier Europe than ever before. For the first time practically all the great peoples will have sorted themselves out, like to like; and it may be assumed that all dynasties hostile to that healthy process will have disappeared. Then, after the attainment of civic freedom and national solidarity, the national instinct, which strengthens with opposition and weakens after due satisfaction, ought to merge in the wider and nobler sentiment of human brotherhood in the attainment of which it is only a preparatory phase.

Printed in the United States of America.

The Heritage of Tyre

By WILLIAM BROWN MELONEY

The Fork of the Road

By WASHINGTON GLADDEN

THE MACMILLAN COMPANY

The Heritage of Tyre

By WILLIAM BROWN MELONEY

Once our flag was known in every part and our keels traversed every sea; all the whalers of the world came out of New Bedford then, and, " Salem " on a ship's stem was as familiar a sight as " Liverpool " is to-day — but those times are gone — forever ? The Yankee clippers will never come back, but William Brown Meloney shows how we can restore the stars and stripes to the seven seas and the prestige of the world's greatest merchant marine to the American people.

"An opportunity to recover our sea heritage stands forth," he writes, "an opportunity of half a world at war — such an opportunity as, in all likelihood, will never present itself again under similar circumstances. We are at peace, we have the necessary maritime genius, we have in abundance the natural resources, to found and maintain a merchant marine. Either wit shall seize this opportunity forthwith, or else our sea folly of the past will continue a hostage to the future, to be delivered only, if at all, by the edge of a crimson sword."

The Forks of the Road

By WASHINGTON GLADDEN

Can a nation lead except by war ? That is the question which faces the United States to-day. Two paths are open, and Washington Gladden has written a book forcefully stating his conviction of which we must choose. Our example is of greater value than our threats; our position demands that we stand firm for peace. The author points out that the present universal desire for peace, expressed in the utterances of every nation, the ultimate beliefs of every religion, the hope and prayer of every individual, needs a leader in the church and an exponent in America.

"If each nation insists on continuing to be a law unto itself and on making its own interests supreme and paramount, the natural reactions will ensue, retribution will repeat itself, and the same dreadful harvesting — only more dire and more universal — will be ready for the reaper before the end of another generation."

THE MACMILLAN COMPANY

Publishers   **64-66 Fifth Avenue**   **New York**

The Pentecost of Calamity

By OWEN WISTER

"One of the most striking and moving utterances. . . . Let all Americans read it." — *The Congregationalist.*

"It is written with sustained charm and freshness of insight." — *New York Times.*

"It is a flaming thing, itself a tongue of Pentecost." — *Boston Advertiser.*

"Mr. Wister's artistic power at its best." — *Philadelphia Ledger.*

"A strong book which sets out to be just a passionate plea to America to find its own soul." — Rabbi STEPHEN S. WISE.

"In 'The Pentecost of Calamity' Owen Wister sees and speaks as a prophet. With rare spiritual insight and sympathy he penetrates to the real meaning of the world tragedy under whose shadow we are living. I am glad we have an American writer able to speak the voiceless longing of an awakened world." — Rev. CHARLES A. EATON, Pastor of the Madison Avenue Baptist Church.

Leaves From a Field Note-Book

By J. H. MORGAN

Late Home Office Commissioner with the British Expeditionary Force

An unofficial outcome of the writer's experiences during the five months he was attached to the British General Headquarters Staff. His official duties during that period involved daily visits to the headquarters of almost every corps, division, and brigade in the field, and took him on several occasions to the batteries and into the trenches. Mr. Morgan has written with spirit and sympathy of the pathetic presence of human emotion amidst the cogs of the machinery of war.

THE MACMILLAN COMPANY

Publishers   64–66 Fifth Avenue   New York

Roadside Glimpses of the Great War

By ARTHUR SWEETSER

Ill., cloth, 12mo, $1.25

Mr. Sweetser's experiences as prisoner of both the Germans and the French are perhaps the most exciting adventures any American has yet described. His book is not a grim, depressing picture of war, but a real, human account of the great conflict, exhilarating in its graphic pictures of the armies and full of many thrilling and humorous episodes.

"A valuable, stirring tale of adventure."— *Boston Transcript*.

"Few equally thrilling stories of personal experiences have been published."—*Bellman*.

"A vivid picture."—*N. Y. Post*.

"Will enthrall the reader from the first page to the last."—*Pittsburgh Dispatch*.

THE MACMILLAN COMPANY
Publishers   64–66 Fifth Avenue   New York

The Diplomacy of the Great War

By ARTHUR BULLARD

Cloth, 12mo, $1.50

A book which contributes to an understanding of the war by revealing something of the diplomatic negotiations that preceded it. The author gives the history of international politics in Europe since the Congress of Berlin in 1878, and considers the new ideals that have grown up about the function of diplomacy during the last generation, so that the reader is in full possession of the general trend of diplomatic development. There is added a chapter of constructive suggestions in respect to the probable diplomatic settlements resulting from the war, and a consideration of the relations between the United States and Europe.

THE MACMILLAN COMPANY

Publishers   64–66 Fifth Avenue   New York